FRANCIS FRITH'S
TOWN & CITY
MEMORIES

DEVIZES

DEE LA VARDERA is a local historian, writer and photographer. This is her sixth book for The Francis Frith Collection on Wiltshire towns and she has also written features about the county and its people for 'Wiltshire Life', 'Farmers Weekly' and 'The Lady'. Originally from Birmingham, Dee came to work in Calne, Wiltshire in 1971 where she taught English until retiring in 2000. She divides her time now between freelance writing and part-time work for Age Concern Wiltshire, based in Devizes.

THE MARKET PLACE c1955 D28053

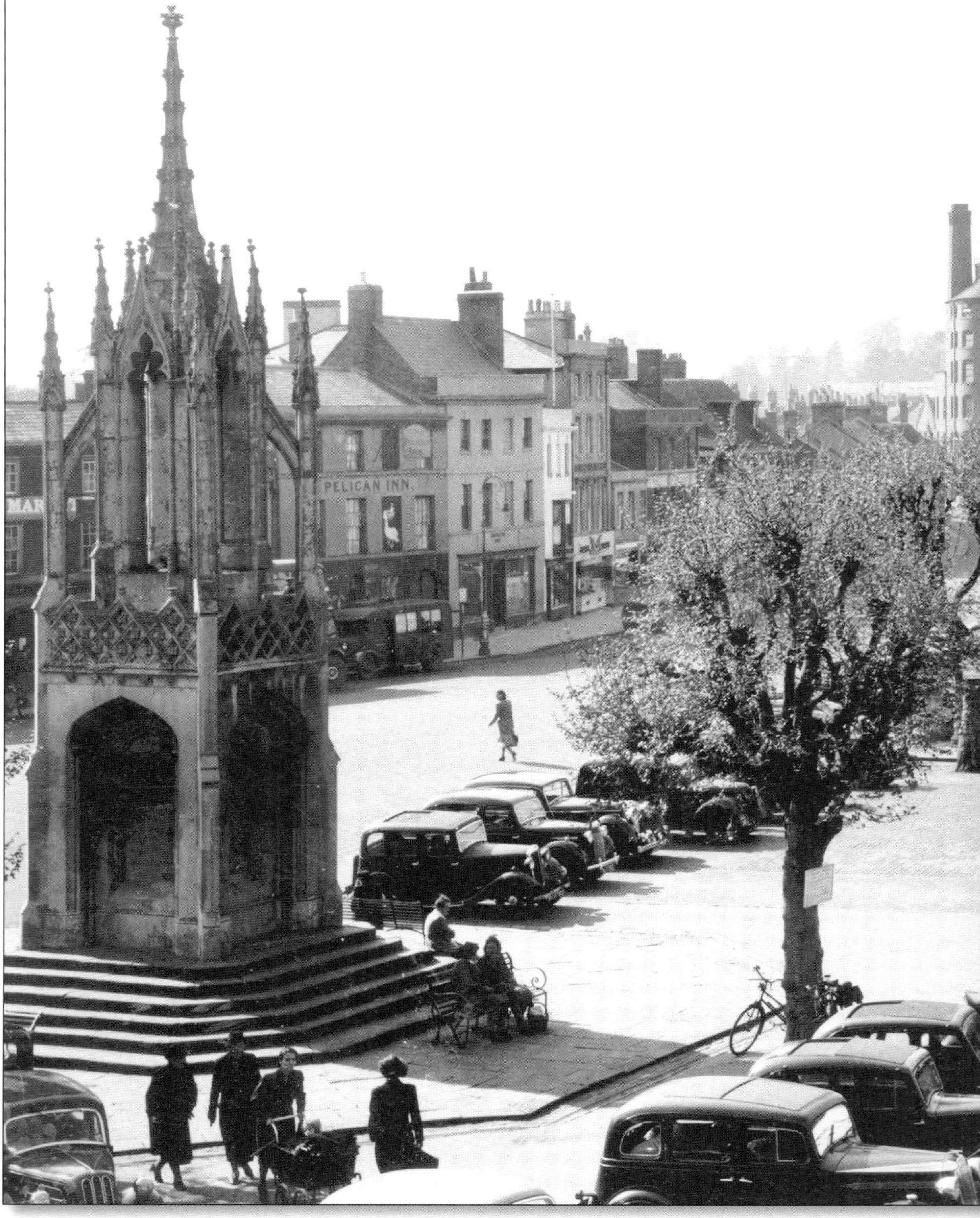

FRANCIS FRITH'S
TOWN & CITY
MEMORIES

DEVIZES

DEE LA VARDERA

FRANCIS FRITH'S
TOWN & CITY
MEMORIES

First published as Devizes, A Photographic History of your Town
in 2001 by Black Horse Books, an imprint of The Francis Frith Collection
Revised edition published in the United Kingdom in 2005 by
The Francis Frith Collection as Devizes, Town and City Memories
Limited Hardback Edition ISBN 1-84589-065-5
Paperback Edition ISBN 1-84589-034-5

British Library Cataloguing in Publication Data

Devizes
Town and City Memories
Dee La Vardera

The Francis Frith Collection®
Frith's Barn, Teffont,
Salisbury, Wiltshire SP3 5QP
Tel: +44 (0) 1722 716 376
Email: info@francisfrith.co.uk
www.francisfrith.co.uk

Aerial photographs reproduced under licence from Simmons Aerofilms Limited
Historical Ordnance Survey maps reproduced under licence from Homecheck.co.uk

Printed and bound in England

Front Cover: **DEVIZES, THE MARKET PLACE c1955** D28072t
The colour-tinting in this image is for illustrative purposes only, and is not intended to be historically accurate

Every attempt has been made to contact copyright holders of illustrative material. We will be happy to give full acknowledgement in future editions for any items not credited. Any information should be directed to The Francis Frith Collection.

AS WITH ANY HISTORICAL DATABASE, THE FRANCIS FRITH ARCHIVE IS CONSTANTLY BEING CORRECTED AND IMPROVED, AND THE PUBLISHERS WOULD WELCOME INFORMATION ON OMISSIONS OR INACCURACIES

ACKNOWLEDGEMENTS

Particular thanks to Dr Lorna Haycock, Sandell Librarian, Wiltshire Heritage Museum, for her knowledge and assistance with the original text.
Thanks to Wiltshire County Library and Wiltshire Gazette & Herald for the use of advertisements and news items.
Thanks also to Barry Barrett, David Buxton, John Girvan, Clive Hackford, Michael Marshman, Jonathan Montagu-Pollock and Alastair Simms for their help.

FRANCIS FRITH'S

TOWN & CITY

MEMORIES

CONTENTS

THE MAKING OF AN ARCHIVE

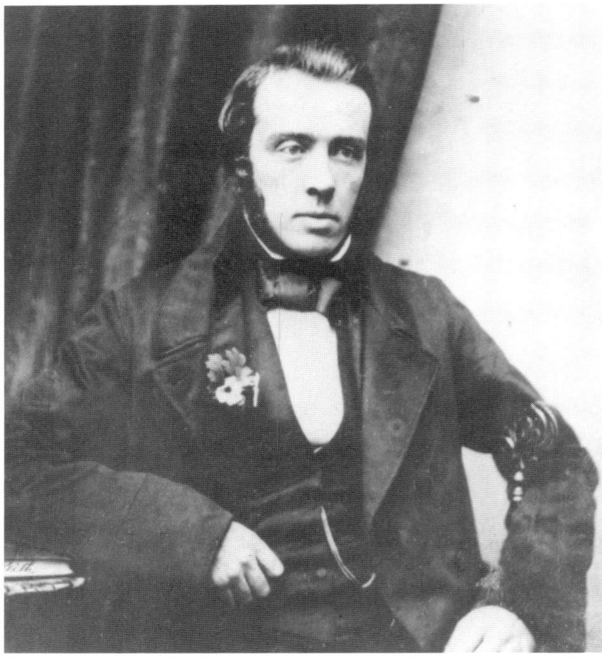

Francis Frith, Victorian founder of the world-famous photographic archive, was a devout Quaker and a highly successful Victorian businessman. By 1860 he was already a multi-millionaire, having established and sold a wholesale grocery business in Liverpool. He had also made a series of pioneering photographic journeys to the Nile region. The images he returned with were the talk of London. An eminent modern historian has likened their impact on the population of the time to that on our own generation of the first photographs taken on the surface of the moon.

Frith had a passion for landscape, and was as equally inspired by the countryside of Britain as he was by the desert regions of the Nile. He resolved to set out on a new career and to use his skills with a camera. He established a business in Reigate as a specialist publisher of topographical photographs.

Frith lived in an era of immense and sometimes violent change. For the poor in the early part of Victoria's reign work was a drudge and the hours long, and ordinary people had precious little free time. Most had not travelled far beyond the boundaries of their own town or village. Mass tourism was in its infancy during the 1860s, but during the next decade the railway network and the establishment of Bank Holidays and half-Saturdays gradually made it possible for the working man and his family to enjoy holidays and to see a little more of the world. With characteristic business acumen, Francis Frith foresaw that these new tourists would enjoy having souvenirs to commemorate their days out. He began selling photo-souvenirs of seaside resorts and beauty spots, which the Victorian public pasted into treasured family albums.

Frith's aim was to photograph every town and village in Britain. For the next thirty years he travelled the country by train and by pony and trap, producing fine photographs of seaside resorts and beauty spots that were keenly bought by millions of Victorians.

THE RISE OF FRITH & CO

Each photograph was taken with tourism in mind, the small team of Frith photographers concentrating on busy shopping streets, beaches, seafronts, picturesque lanes and villages. They also photographed buildings: the Victorian and Edwardian eras were times of huge building activity, and town halls, libraries, post offices, schools and technical colleges were springing up all over the country. They were invariably celebrated by a proud Victorian public, and photo souvenirs – visual records – published by F Frith & Co were sold in their hundreds of thousands. In addition, many new commercial buildings such as hotels, inns and pubs were photographed, often because their owners specifically commissioned Frith postcards or prints of them for re-sale or for publicity purposes.

In order to gain some understanding of the scale of Frith's business one only has to look at the catalogue issued by Frith & Co in 1886: it runs to some 670 pages. By 1890 Frith had created the greatest specialist photographic publishing company in the world, with over 2,000 stockists! The picture on the right shows the Frith & Co display board on the wall of the stockist at Ingleton in the Yorkshire Dales (left of window). Beautifully constructed with a mahogany frame and gilt inserts, it displayed a dozen scenes.

THE MAKING OF AN ARCHIVE

POSTCARD BONANZA

The ever-popular holiday postcard we know today took many years to appear, and F Frith & Co was in the vanguard of its development. Postcards became a hugely popular means of communication and sold in their millions. Frith's company took full advantage of this boom and soon became the major publisher of photographic view postcards.

Francis Frith died in 1898 at his villa in Cannes, his great project still growing. His sons Eustace and Cyril continued their father's monumental task, expanding the number of views offered to the public and recording more and more places in Britain, as the coasts and countryside were opened up to mass travel. The archive Frith created continued in business for another seventy years. By 1970 it contained over a third of a million pictures of 7,000 cities, towns and villages. The massive photographic record Frith has left to us stands as a living monument to a special and very remarkable man.

This book shows Devizes as it was photographed by this world-famous archive at various periods in its development over the past 150 years. Every photograph was taken for a specific commercial purpose, which explains why the selection may not show every aspect of the town landscape. However, the photographs, compiled from one of the world's most celebrated archives, provide an important and absorbing record of your town.

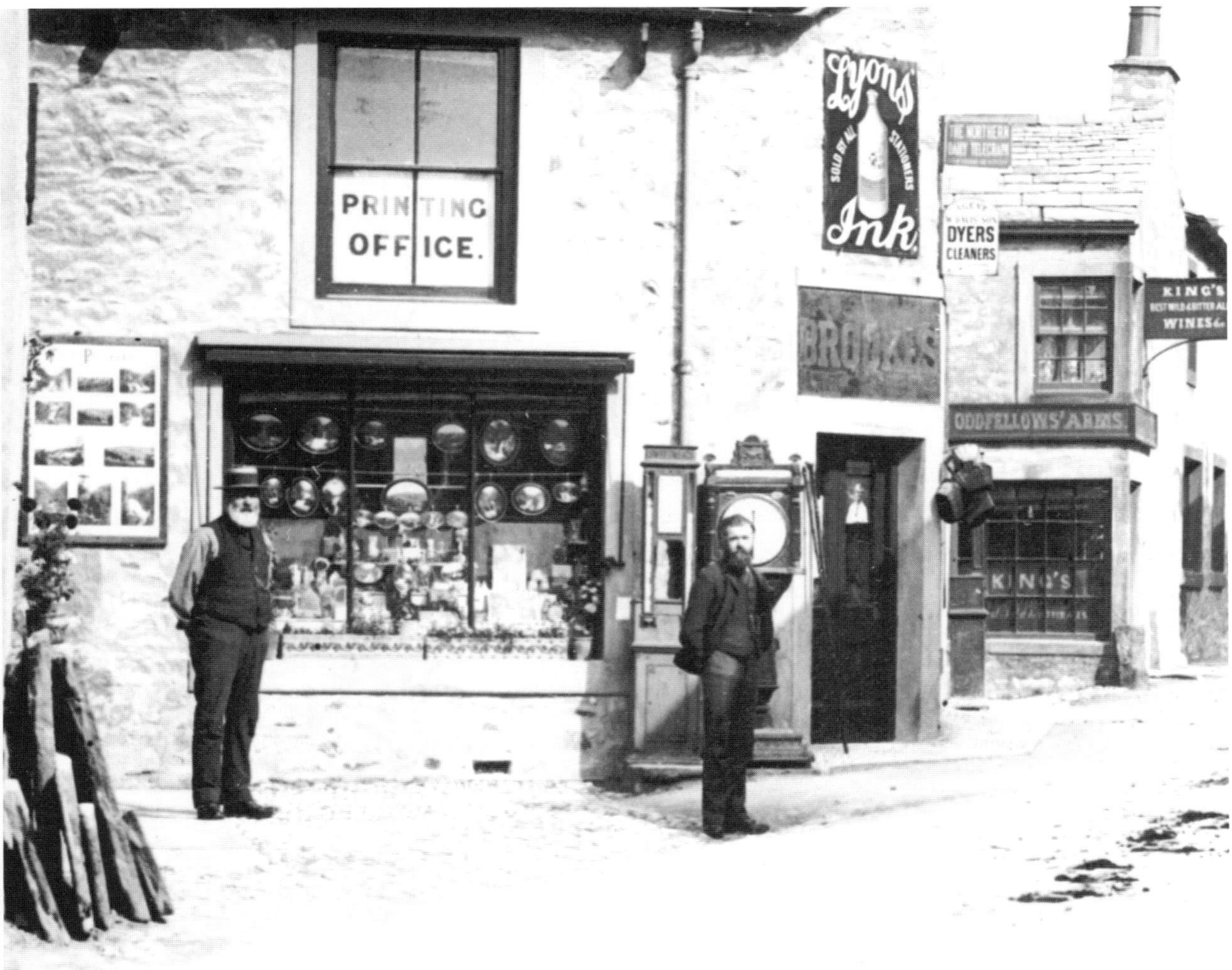

FROM THE AIR

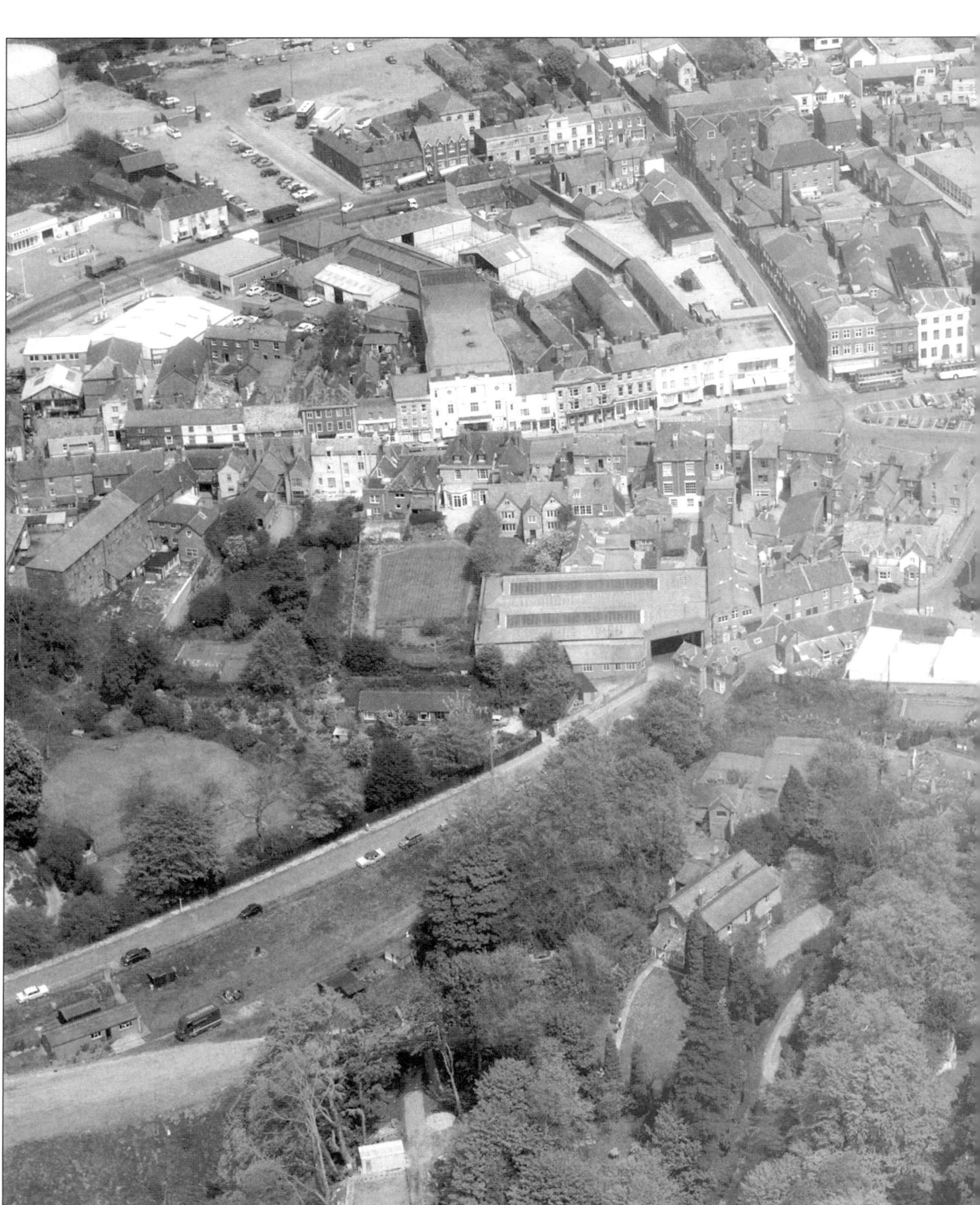

DEVIZES FROM THE AIR

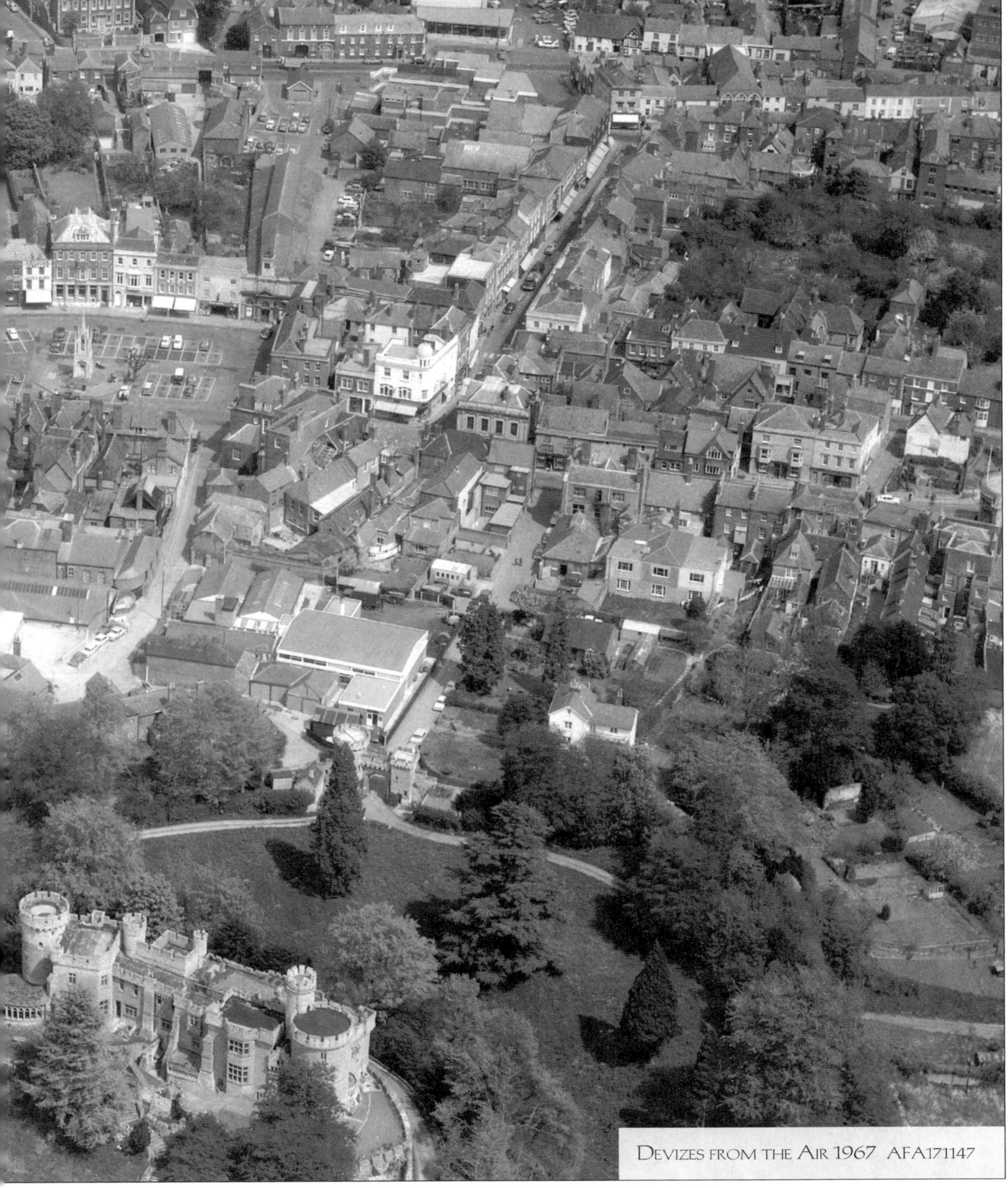

Devizes from the Air 1967 AFA171147

INTRODUCTION

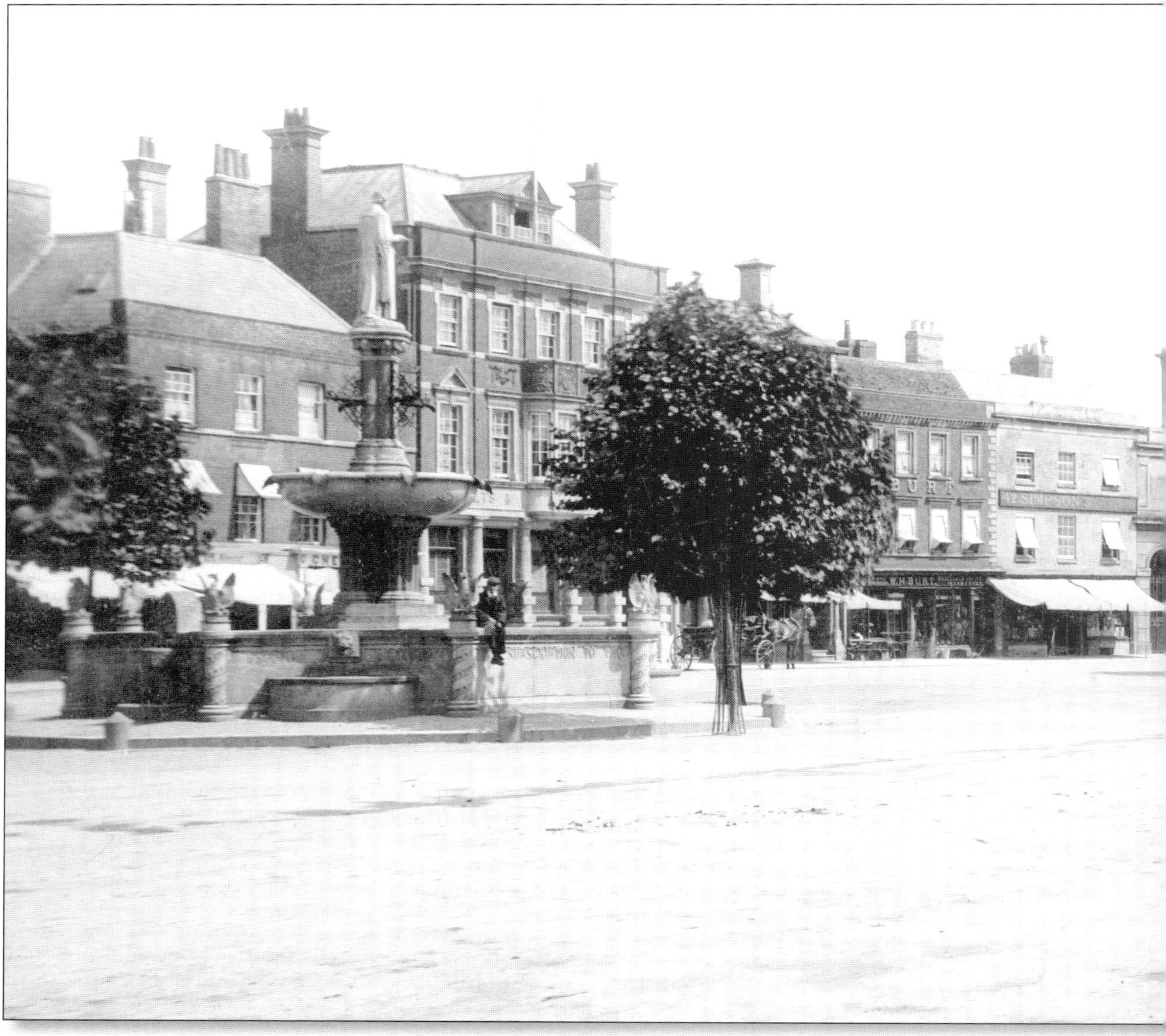

Devizes, situated in the beautiful vale of Pewsey, is one of the gems in Wiltshire's crown. It sits upon a ledge at the western base of the Marlborough Downs. It was described by A G Bradley in his 'Round About Wiltshire' in 1928 as 'a pleasant, old-fashioned, sunny-looking town, not to say a windy one, being five hundred feet above sea-level, and exposed to all the breezes that blow'. Its position on the A4 London to Bristol road makes it well-placed for visiting such historic sites as Stonehenge, Avebury and Bath. The tradition of visitors regularly passing through the town is an old one: Devizes was once on the main coaching route from Bath to London in the 18th century.

It is a town of historical and architectural interest. Its early fortunes were founded on the woollen trade and the tobacco industry, and many of the buildings reflect the commercial and domestic wealth of its early clothiers, factory owners and traders. It has one of the largest concentrations of historic buildings in the country: there are nearly five hundred structures which have been listed, and are therefore

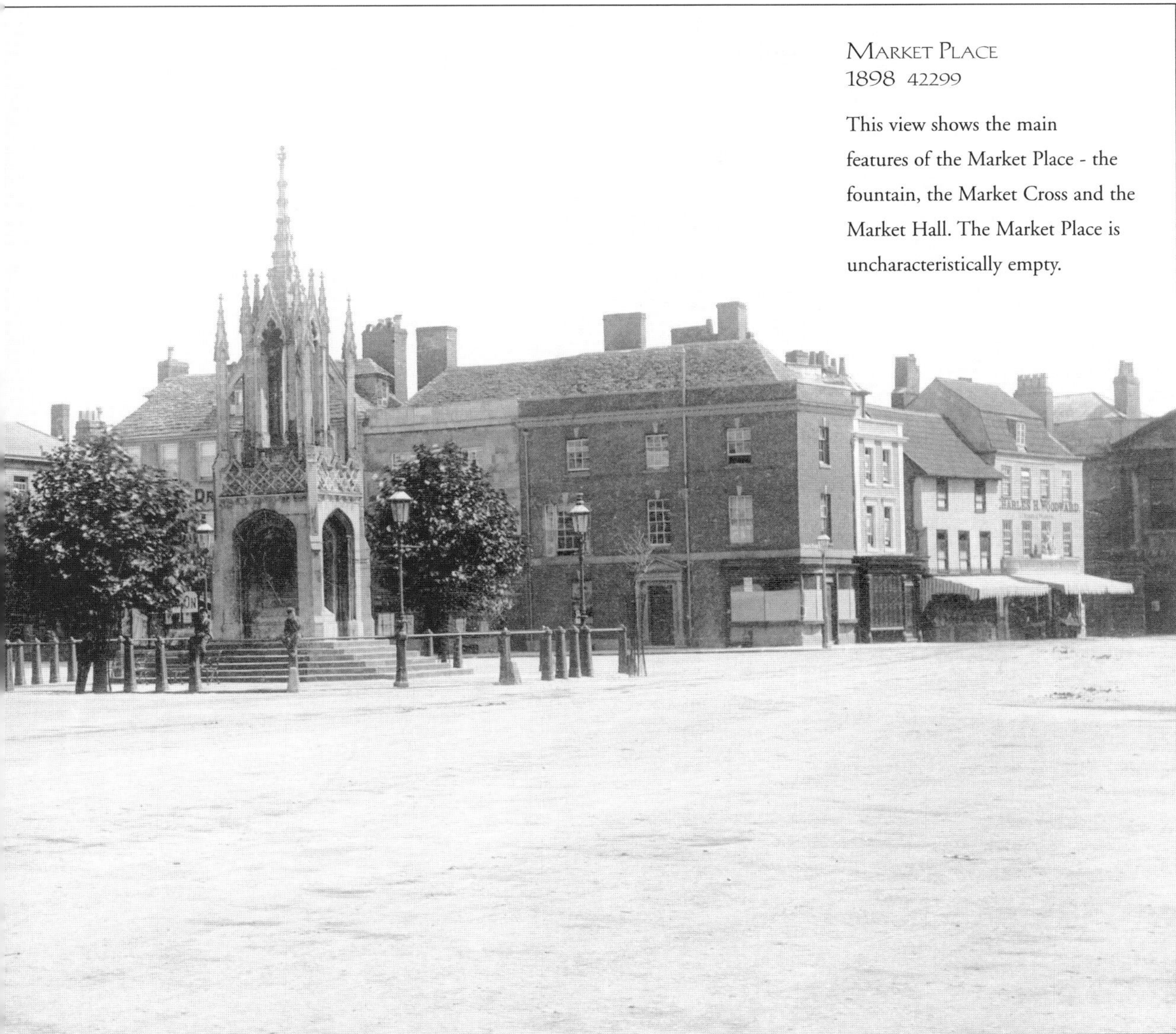

MARKET PLACE
1898 42299

This view shows the main features of the Market Place - the fountain, the Market Cross and the Market Hall. The Market Place is uncharacteristically empty.

protected by the Department of the Environment. The town has changed little physically; not one new major street line has been created in over eight hundred years.

Today, Devizes is a busy working community, still retaining the tradition of its 850-year-old street market. The town has avoided being swamped by large supermarket chains, and there are still a number of small independent traders. It has moved firmly into the 21st century by continuing its tradition of encouraging new businesses. A wide range of products is produced here, from beer and cardboard boxes to the safety harnesses used on Sydney Harbour Bridge. Among the town's biggest employers are Hayden's bakery which supplies major supermarket chains, Omitec which produces diagnostic equipment for automobiles, and T H White, agricultural engineering company, which has its HQ in Nursteed Road. Also the new Wiltshire Emergency Communications Centre based at Wiltshire Constabulary HQ, London Road, became fully operational in March 2004 with over 160 staff from the police, fire and ambulance services.

BISHOPS AND BOROUGHS

THE CASTLE 1898
42309

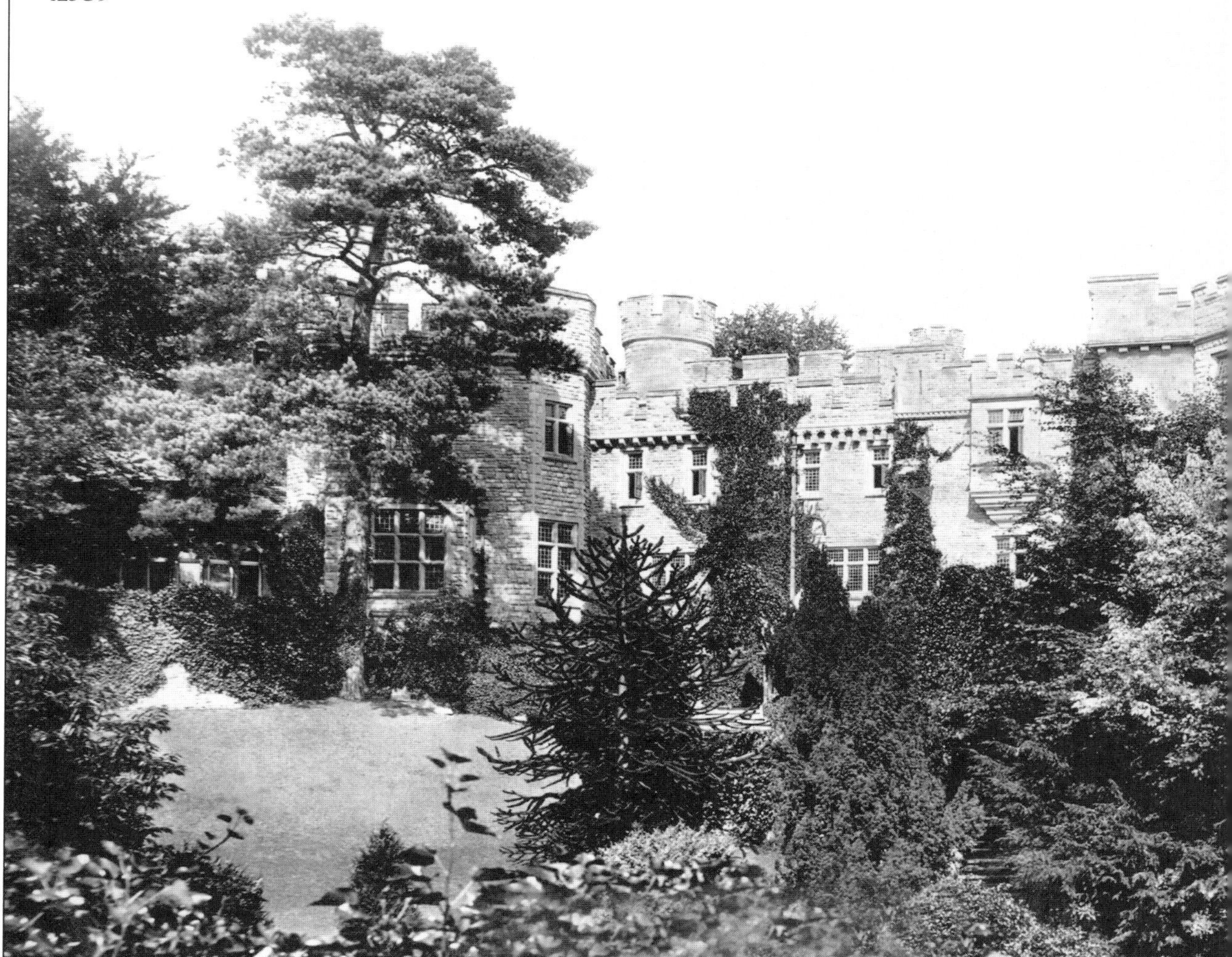

There is no mention of the town in the Domesday Book (1086), but there may have been fortified earthworks here in ancient times. Roman coins and artefacts have been unearthed, so undoubtedly there was a Roman settlement. The town's name is thought to come from the Latin words 'ad divisas', or their Old French equivalent 'les diveses', meaning 'on the boundaries'. This referred to the position of the castle on the boundaries of the Bishop of Salisbury's manors of Rowde, Cannings and Potterne. By the 14th century the first syllable was often dropped, and the town was known until quite recent times as 'Vyse' or 'the Vyse'.

Devizes originally had a wooden castle, which was built by Osmund, Bishop of Salisbury soon after the Norman Conquest. It was rebuilt between 1113 and 1120 after a fire. John Leland, the travelling writer in Henry VIII's reign, said 'that such a piece of castle-work, so costly and strongly, was never afore nor since set up by any bishop of England' as Roger, Bishop of Salisbury then built for himself. Roger had started as a humble curate, but was awarded

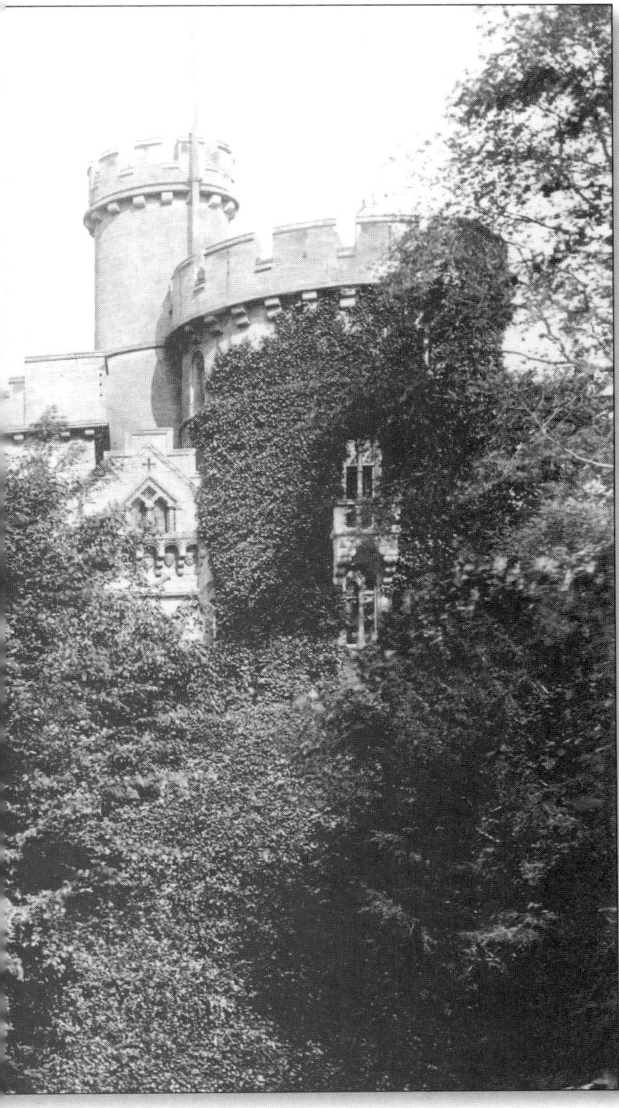

preferments and honours by the young King Henry I. For thirty years the Bishop remained the most powerful man in the land after the King. Whilst Henry was away fighting in Normandy, Roger effectively ruled the country, signing charters 'ex parte regis' (on behalf of the king).

One stormy period in the castle's, and the town's, history occurred during the period when Henry tried to secure the succession for his daughter Matilda, who was also Empress Maud, wife of the Holy Roman Emperor. When Henry died in 1135, his nephew Stephen of Blois returned from France. Having been crowned King, he took Bishop Roger and his son hostages. The castle was surrendered to Stephen, but he was ousted later by Empress Maud and her supporters. Although Maud's rule did not last long, she did have time to issue a number of charters: these included the one which gave exemption to Devizes from 'land-toll, ferry-toll, fair toll, and every other custom', and granted it borough status.

But by 1538 the castle had fallen into ruin. Many of its stones were used to build houses in the town. The site of the present castle was acquired by the Leach family in 1838; they started work on new buildings to designs by H E Goodridge, a prominent Bath builder and architect, who was responsible for Beckford's Lansdown Tower. He abandoned the Greek Revival style of his Bath buildings for the Gothic style which is evident in the round towers, oriel windows and battlement walls.

The basis of the town's wealth was its local industries and market trading. Lorna Haycock writes: 'During the eighteenth century, Devizes became one of the premier corn markets in the kingdom, its prices being regularly quoted in the London newspapers. Cloth making was one of the town's principal industries from as early as the 13th century. There were also glove makers, tanners and metal workers. Devizes people were resourceful, and the variety of work on offer helped the market to expand and the town to prosper. The wool trade continued to flourish into the 18th century, when John Anstie built one of the first factories in the west of England in New Park Street (now converted into flats). We can still see the pulleys for lifting bales up to the upper floors' windows. At one time Anstie had twenty spinning jennies and three hundred weaving looms. Unfortunately, he went bankrupt in 1793, his overseas and London trade having been badly affected by the French War. His brother Benjamin successfully ran a tobacco business which became a major employer for many years, famous for its Gold Flake cigarettes.

Devizes' borough status was lost in 1974 when the 1972 Local Government Act put an end to the Borough Charter which had been granted by Maud in 1141. The town has developed considerably over the centuries. In 1801 the population of Devizes town parish was 3,547, in 1901 it was 6,532 and in 2001 it was 11,296. With boundary changes and new housing developments, the wider Devizes Community Area population in 2004 was 30,020.

CHEESECAKE AND CHOPS

The Market Place is the largest in the west of England. Nearly all the buildings which surround it are listed. The market originally grew up around the castle, with the traders serving the garrison. There is a record of a special licence to trade being granted in 1228. The medieval market took place in the wide space outside St Mary's church before it was developed into the present day Maryport Street and Monday Market Street. The market cross stood at the corner of the White Bear Inn on the corner of Monday Market Street and New Park Street (see D28090, page 48).

John Britton wrote in his 'Beauties of Wiltshire' in 1801 that the Market Place 'is abundantly supplied every Thursday with all kinds of corn, wool, cheese, cattle etc from the adjacent country'. This tradition of trading has served Devizes well, and continues today with its weekly Thursday market and monthly Farmers' market, along with the occasional French one.

As a commercial location, the Market Place attracted a variety of businesses, catering for all classes of people. In 1901 there were two ironmongers, three watchmakers, a rope and basket maker, a gunsmith, a tailor, a shoe maker and even a school for boys, as well as the banks, hotels, greengrocers, bakers, stationers and auctioneers that we find today.

I don't know if Devizes people had a particular problem with their teeth, but the 'Wiltshire Gazette' carried three advertisements in the 19 November 1908 edition for peripatetic dentists based in the Market Place (see page 44845 for advertisements).

View 44845 (page 16-17) shows some of the best architecture in Devizes — and notice how well the styles marry together. On the left is the Market Cross, and behind we can see the imposing front of No 38, The Wilts & Dorset Banking Co Ltd, now Lloyds. It was built in 1892 in an early Georgian style with Portland and Bath stone facings; six Tuscan columns are set dramatically at the front of the five-bay facade. There are attractive floral swags below the windows to either side of the first floor centre window (see also 42300 pages 20-21). No 40, hidden by the trees, is Frank Williams, florist and tomato grower. No 41 is Burt's the ironmonger, and next door is Simpson & Son, tea merchants (see the advertisement on page 18). Far right is the Market Hall, also known as the Shambles.

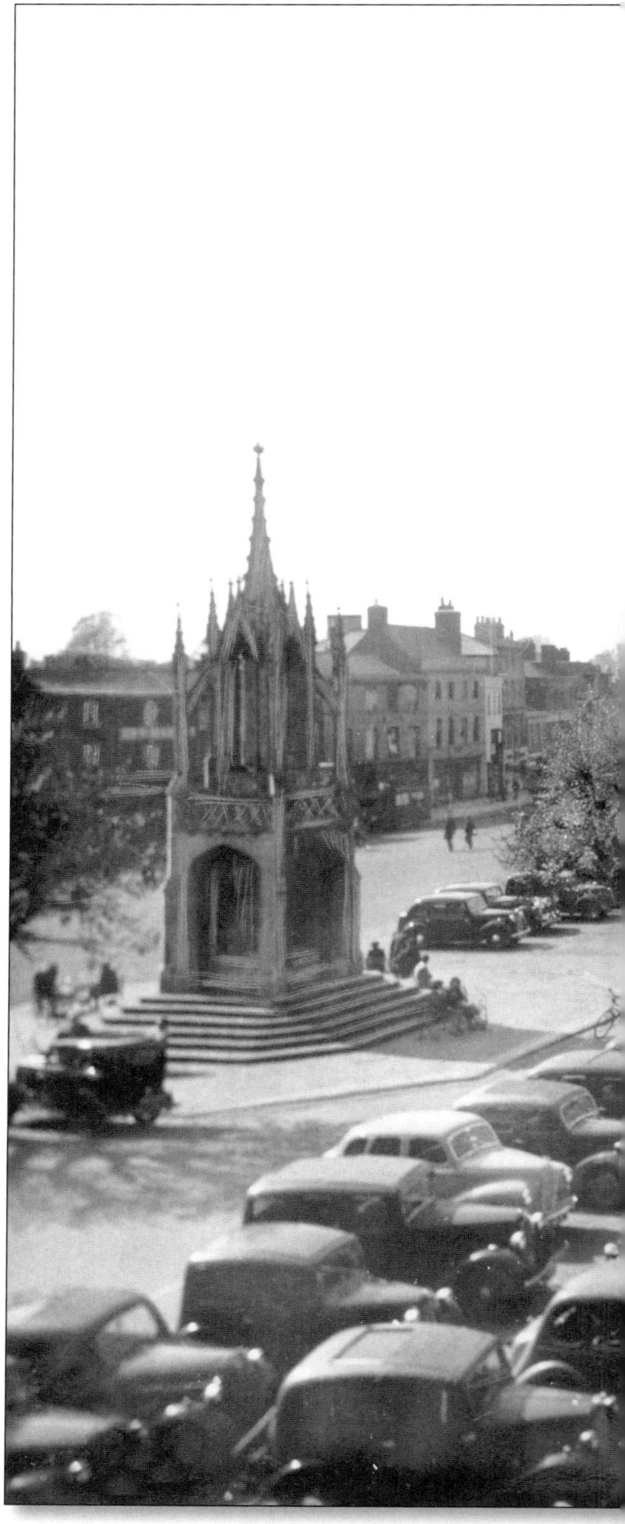

MARKET PLACE c1950 D28052

The present-day Market Place was formed from the outer bailey of the castle. This particular view shows the curve of the street: this echoes the line of New Park Street and Monday Market Street, which follow the castle's banks and ditches. The buildings and shape of the skyline have changed little.

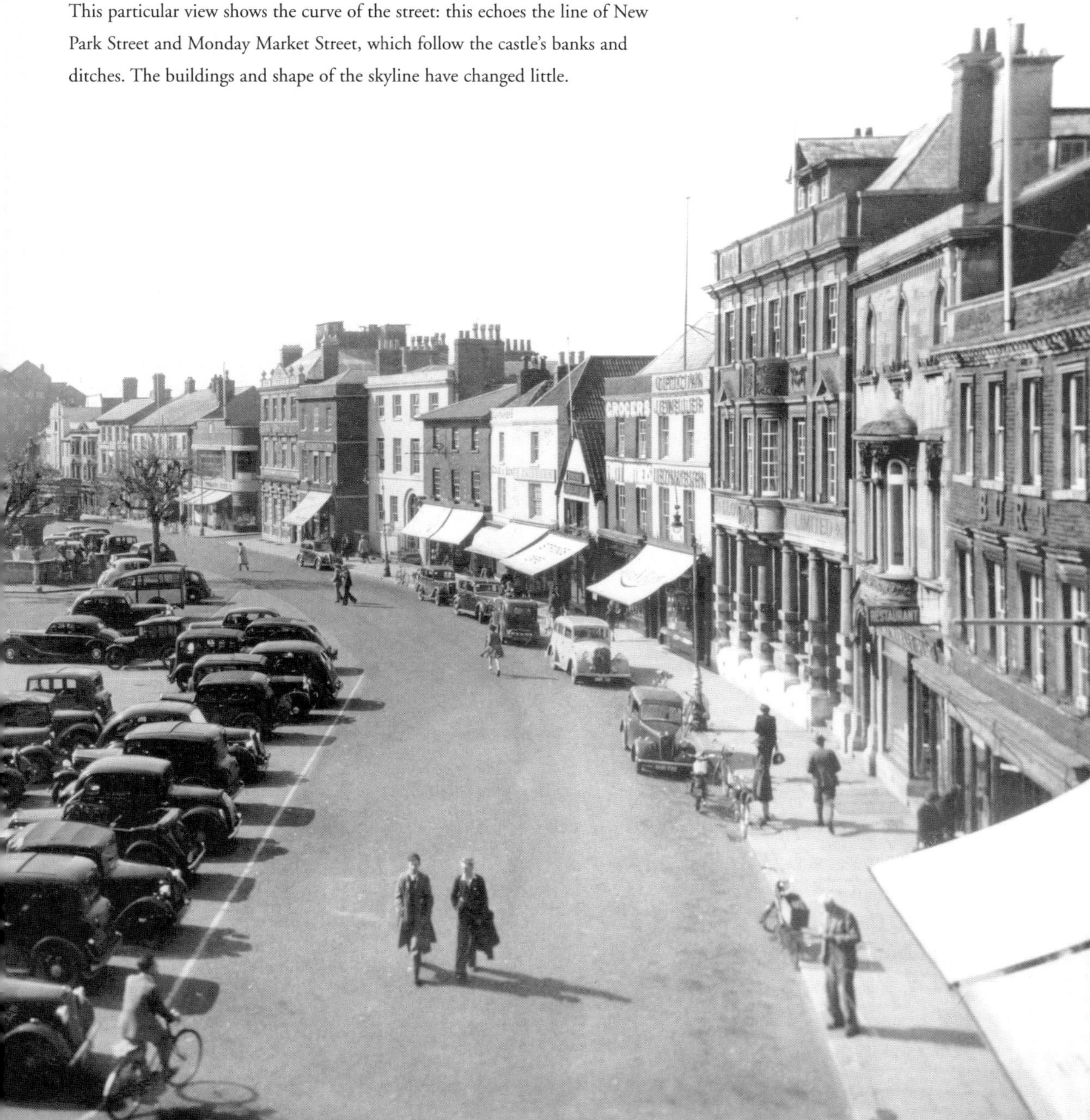

CHEESECAKE AND CHOPS

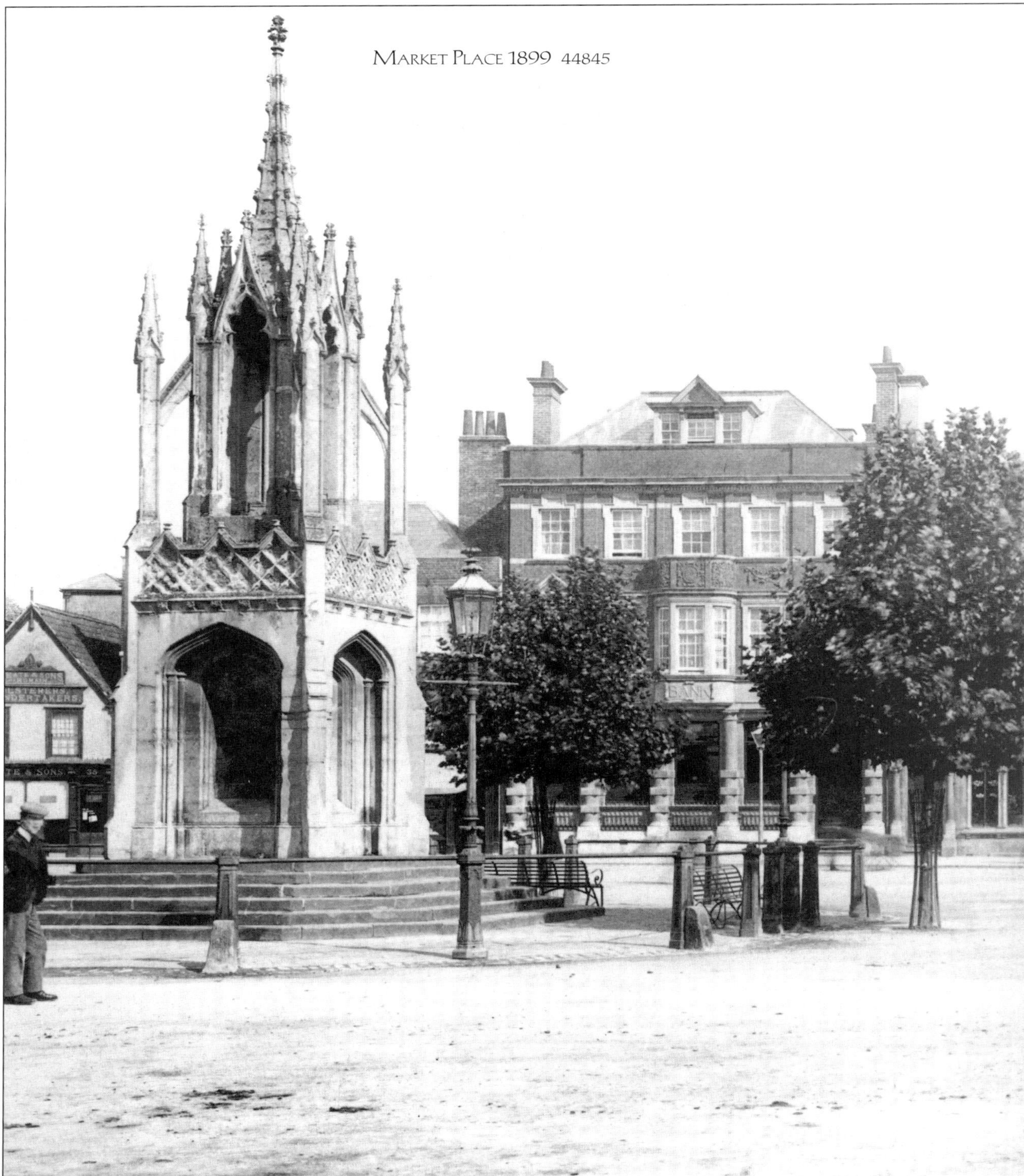

MARKET PLACE 1899 44845

THE MARKET PLACE - EAST SIDE

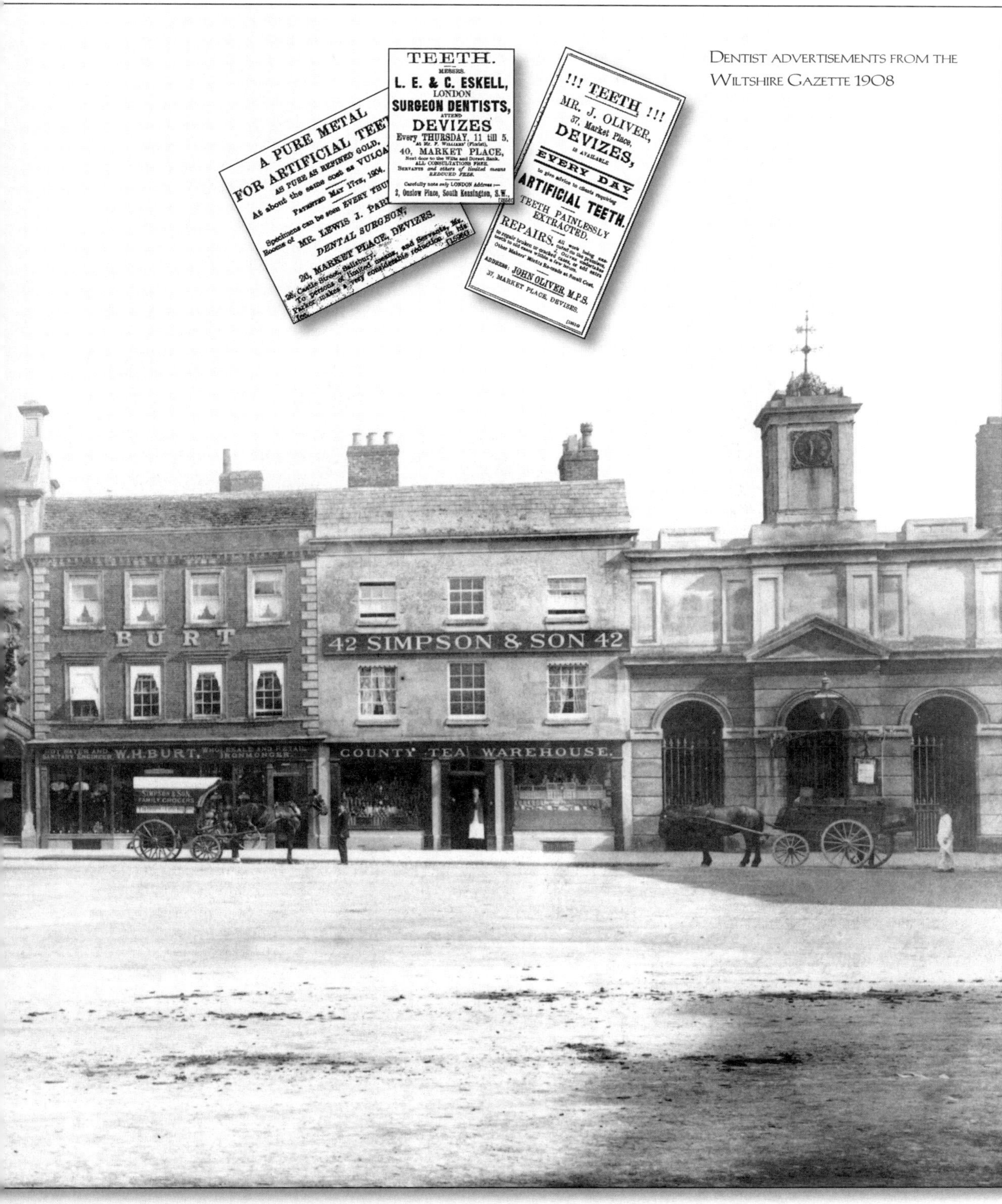

Dentist advertisements from the Wiltshire Gazette 1908

CHEESECAKE AND CHOPS

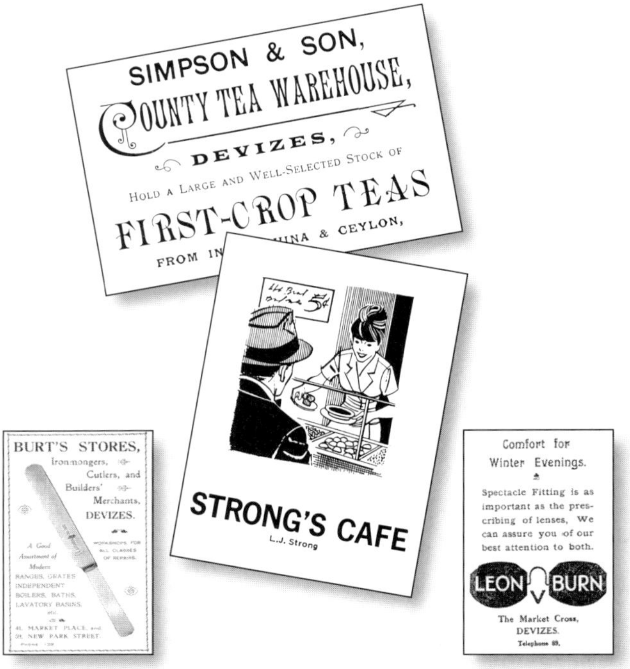

ADVERTISEMENTS FOR SIMPSON & SON, GILLMAN'S DIRECTORY 1901, STRONG'S CAFÉ, DEVIZES AND DISTRICT DIRECTORY 1970, BURT'S STORES, FROM THE OFFICIAL GUIDE TO THE TOWN OF DEVIZES 1931 AND LEON V BURN, FROM PALACE CINEMA PROGRAMME 1938

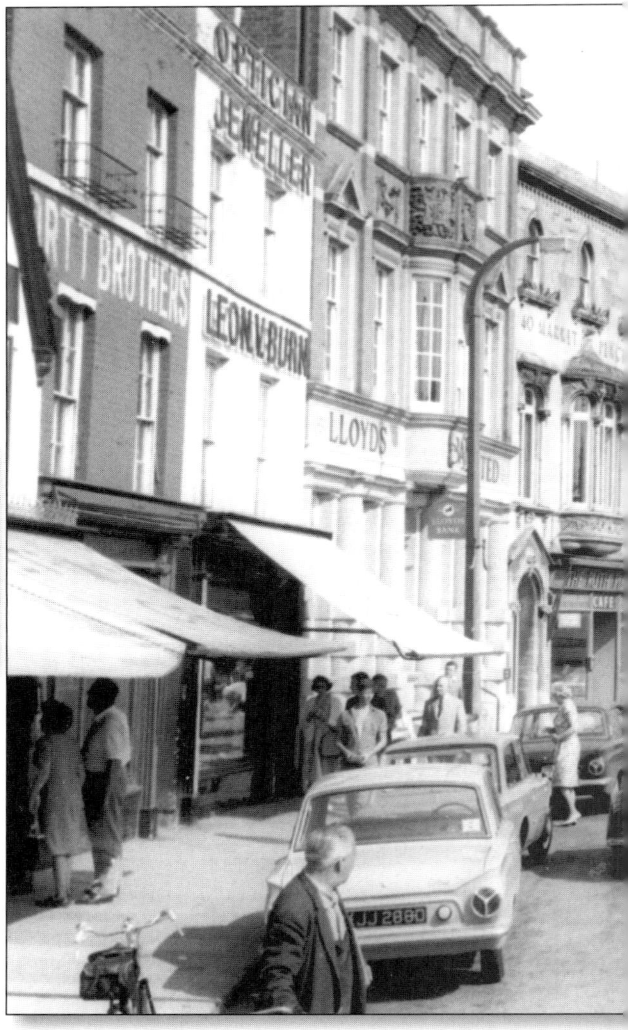

The Market Hall (44845, page 16) was designed by Pollard, an architect from Frome, in 1835 and built in 1838; it replaced a former hall donated in 1791 by Henry Addington, first Viscount Sidmouth. He had been MP from 1784 to 1805, and Prime Minister from 1801 until he was raised to the peerage. It was built on the site of the old butchers' market or shambles, a Middle English word for a place which sells meat or fish.

View D28083 was taken looking towards the Market Hall and Little Brittox. In the extreme left is the sloping pantile roof of Strong's, the bakery and café famous for its Devizes cheesecake. This was made to an original secret recipe by Jonas Strong, formerly of the Brittox. Next is Fortt Brothers, the grocers, now Nationwide, Leon W Burn, optician and jeweller, Lloyds Bank, and then The Borough Restaurant, now Superdrug.

The Market Cross (42300 overleaf) was designed by Benjamin Wyatt with L J Abington in 1814. It is built in Bath stone, and consists of a plain rectangular base with a buttress at each angle crowned with a pinnacle and an octagonal decorated spire. It was erected in 1814 by Henry, 1st Viscount Sidmouth, who was Recorder of the borough for 30 years. He was Prime Minister from 1801 to 1804, and Member of Parliament from 1784 to 1805. There is a remarkable (and lengthy) inscription on the east panel of the Cross, recording an event which occurred in 1753: Ruth Pierce of Potterne was said to have been struck down dead for dishonesty in trading.

THE MARKET PLACE - EAST SIDE

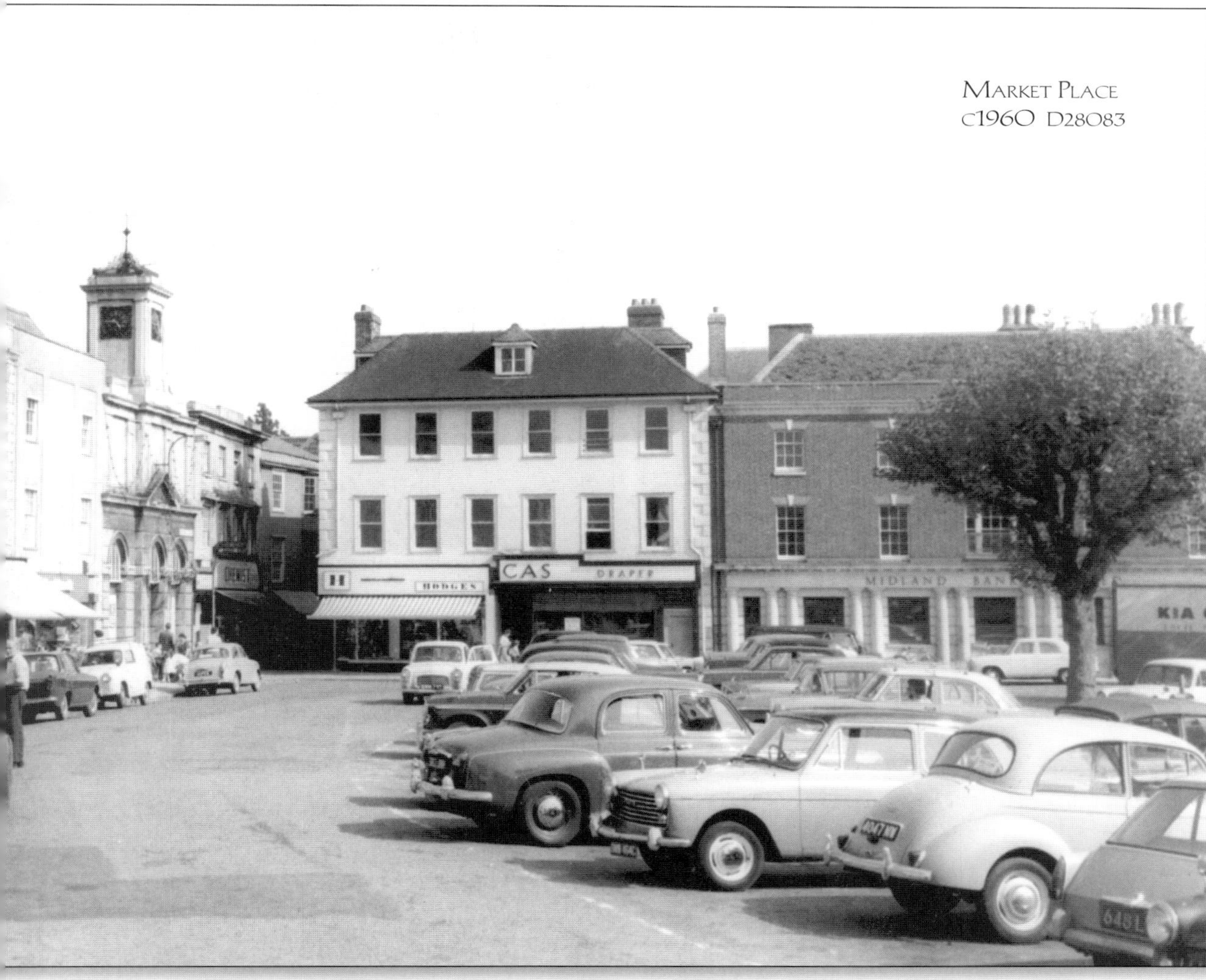

MARKET PLACE
C1960 D28083

The plane trees beside the Market Cross have been regularly pollarded to limit their size. The bollards and lamp posts shown were removed for salvage during the last war. J V Lucas (D28072, page 22, to the right of the Market Cross) was a well-established draper and milliner at the turn of the century, and was known as 'the people's draper'.

The Market Place has always been important to people in the town as a focal point. There was much public outcry and demonstrations when the diseased plane trees were cut down in 2001. The reduction in parking spaces caused by new bus stop areas also changed the appearance.

Even though there are only about five years between D28052 (pages 14-15) and D28084 (page 24), it is interesting to see how markedly different are the models of the cars. The parking problems are just the same now; all we need to do is to change the models again to bring the picture up to the present day.

The fountain was built in 1879 as a memorial to the Rt Hon T H S Sotheron Estcourt, President of the Poor Law Board, founder of the Wiltshire Friendly Society, and MP for Devizes and North Wiltshire. The 'Devizes Advertiser' reported that 'at that time the need of a drinking fountain was felt in the town'. Built in Aberdeen granite, it consists of an octagonal basin with a 50ft-high statue of Mr Sotheron Estcourt rising from the centre. At the base is a drinking fountain and water trough for cattle. Pevsner describes it as

CHEESECAKE AND CHOPS

MARKET CROSS 1898 42300

This view clearly shows the iron benches, railings and posts and the ornate street lamps. The earth road is in marked contrast to today's tarmac surface.

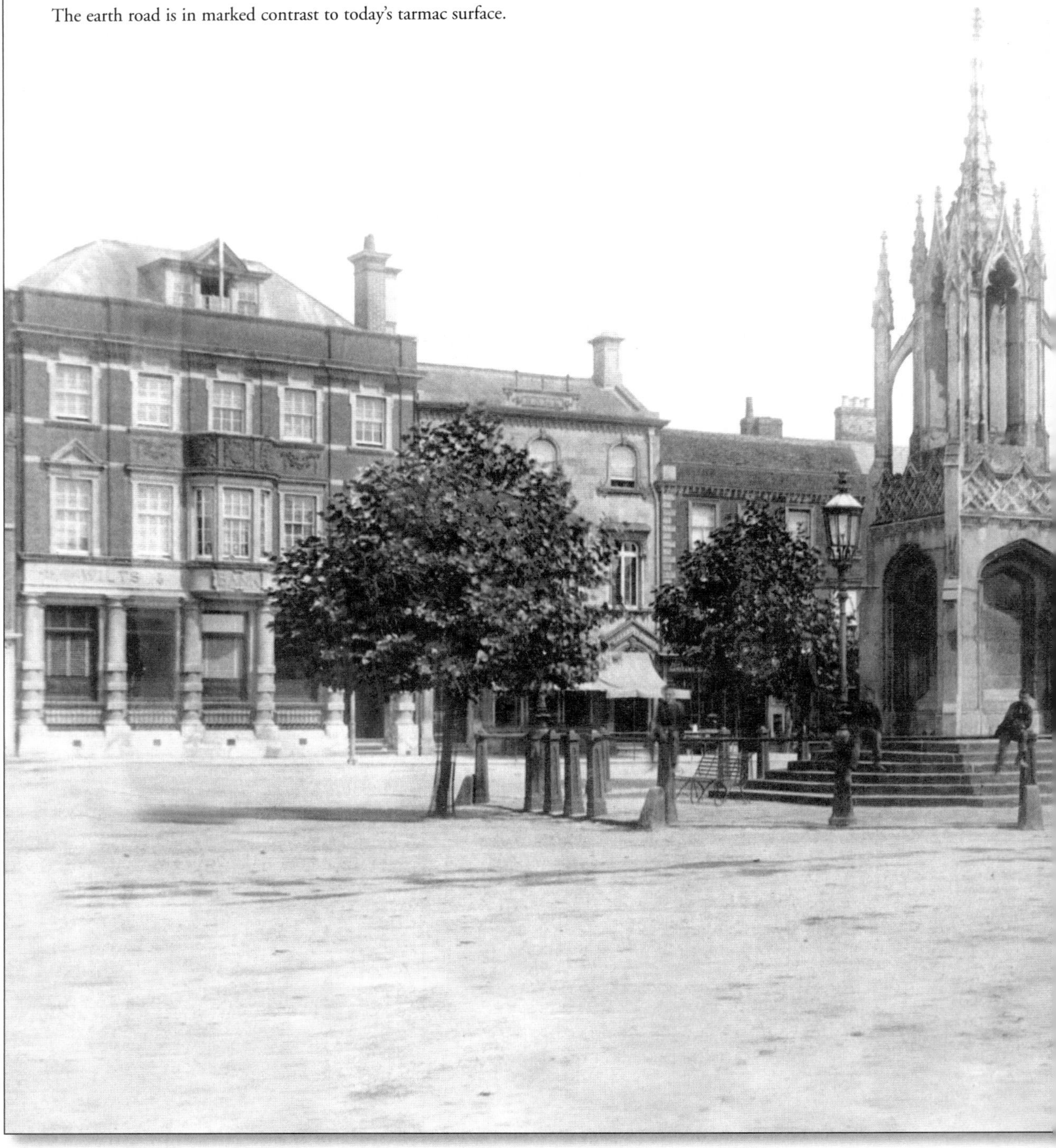

THE MARKET PLACE - EAST SIDE

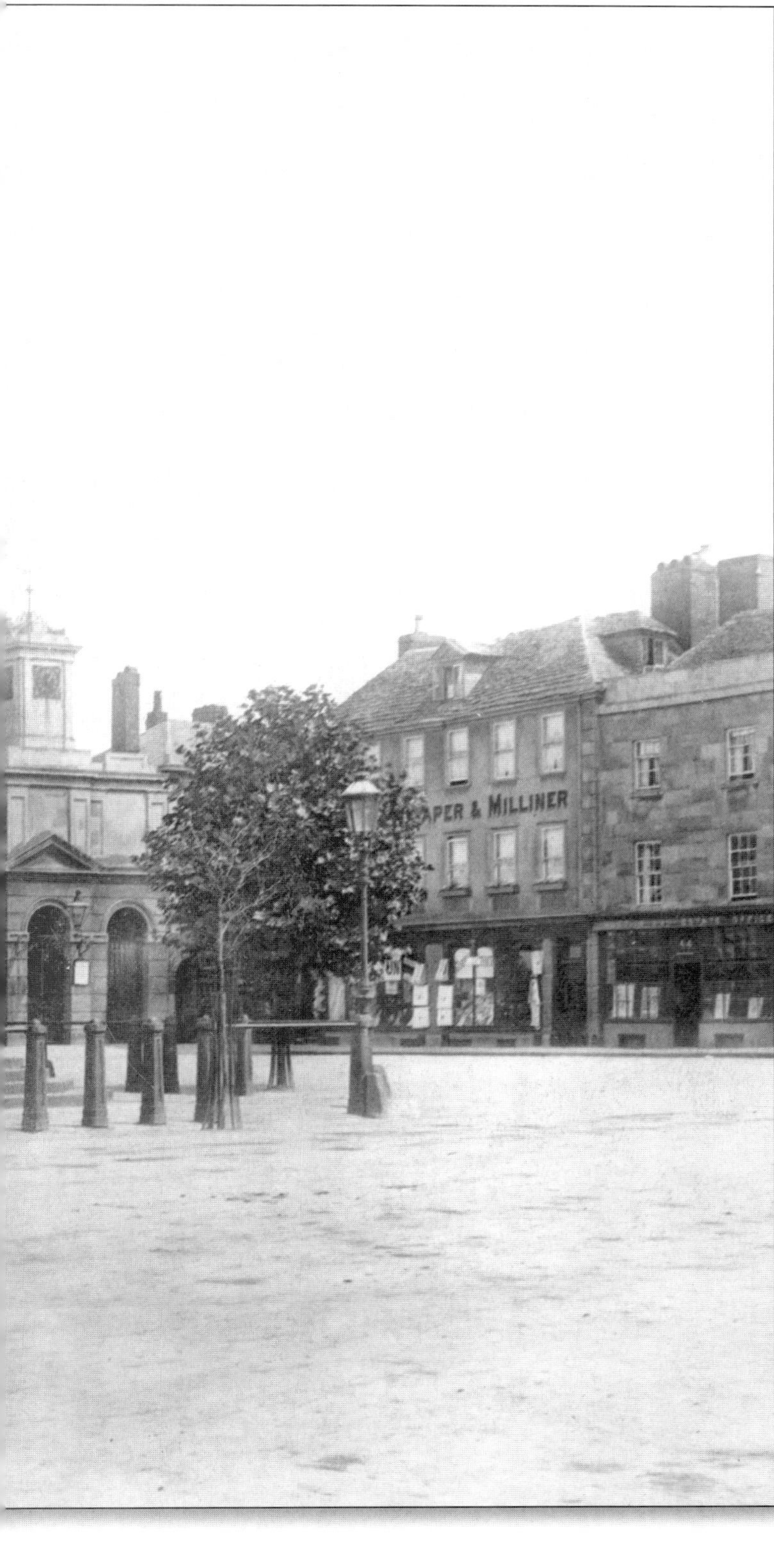

THE MARKET CROSS

The surveyor has received instructions to have the inscription plates on the Cross cleaned, and to procure tenders for re-gilding and re-lettering the inscriptions with the best gold-leaf. He has also requested to obtain a price, from Mr. Jas. Honey (who has the painter's work for the term) for cleaning the lamp posts and pillars and re-painting them in the same style and colours as before.

A notice from the Wiltshire Gazette, 19 March 1908

THE PRIME MINISTER

(THE RT. HON. CLEMENT ATTLEE, C.H.)

will speak in support of WILFRED CAVE

in

DEVIZES MARKET PLACE

on

TUESDAY, OCTOBER 16th

at 3.45 p.m.

A notice from the Wiltshire Gazette, 11 October 1951

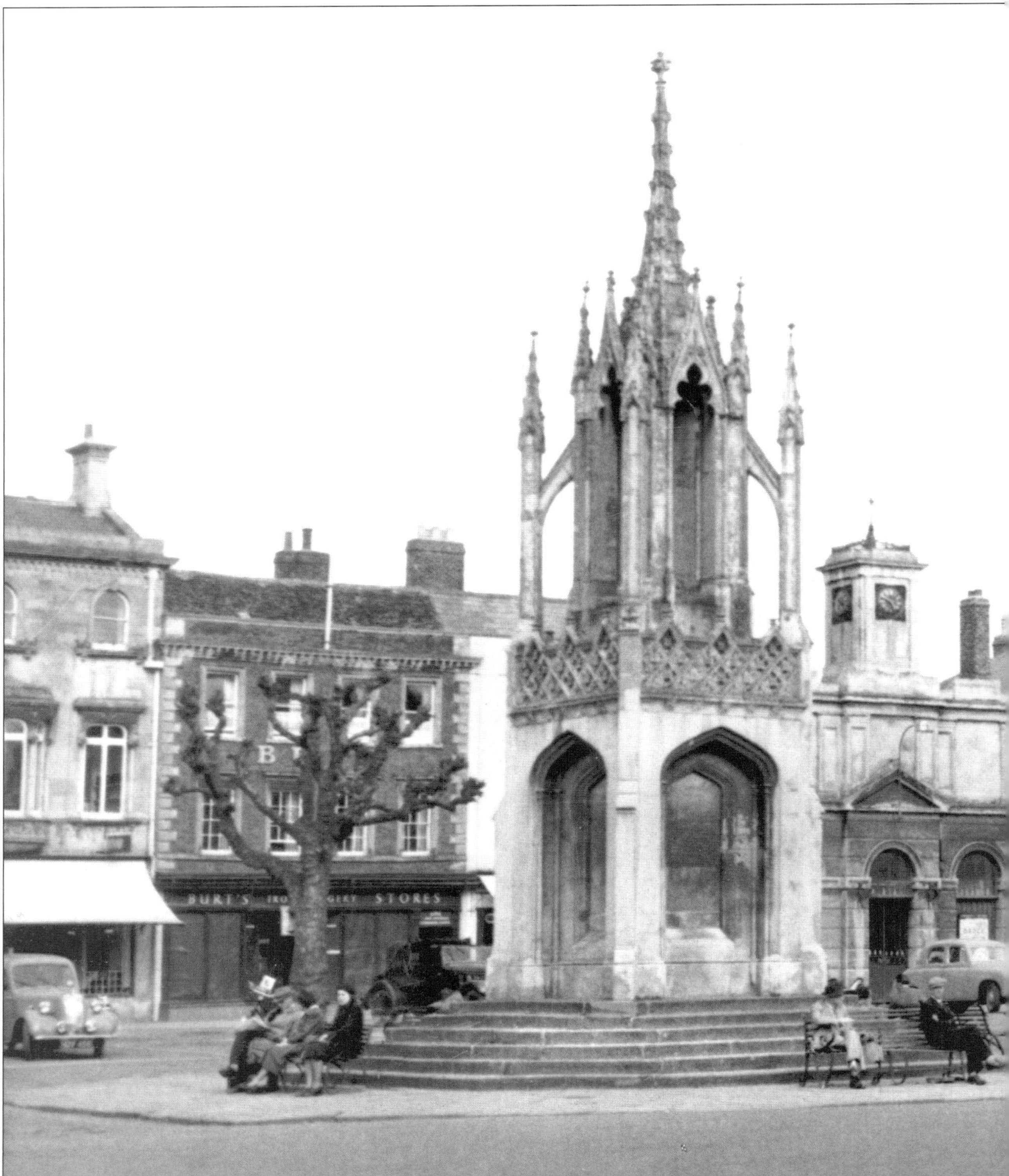
BURT'S
STORES

THE MARKET PLACE - EAST SIDE

MARKET PLACE c1955 D28072

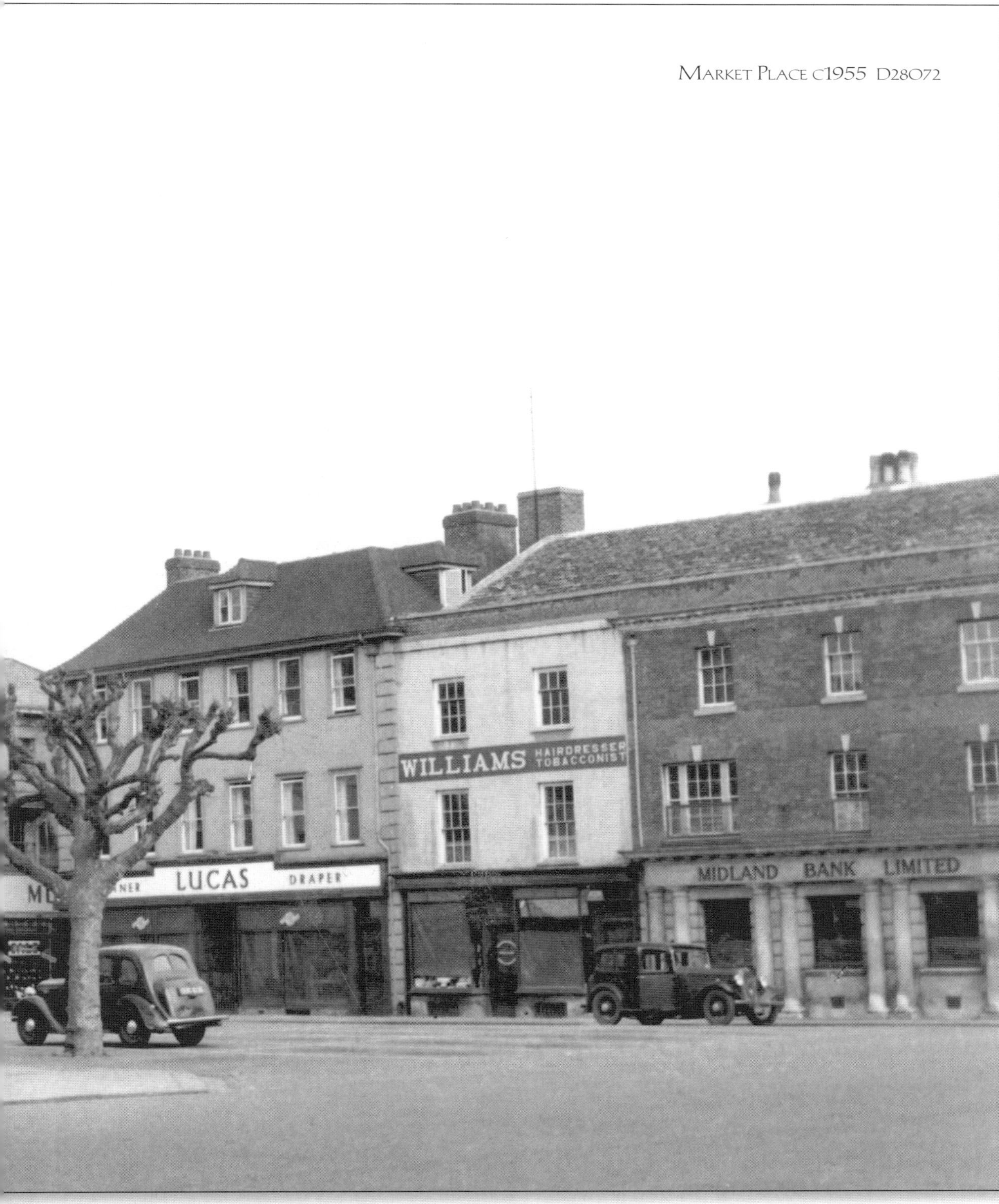

Market Place c1960 D28084

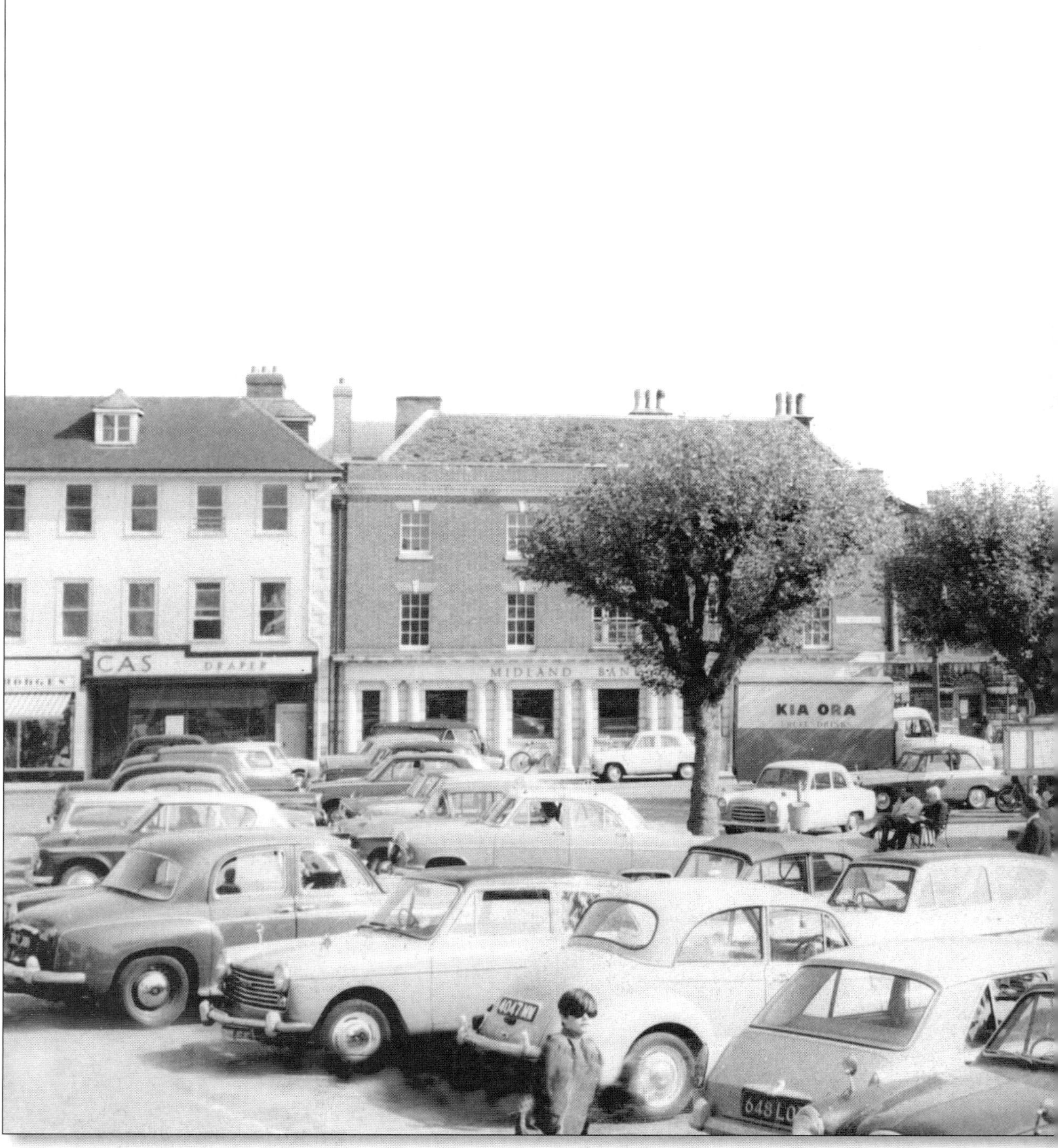

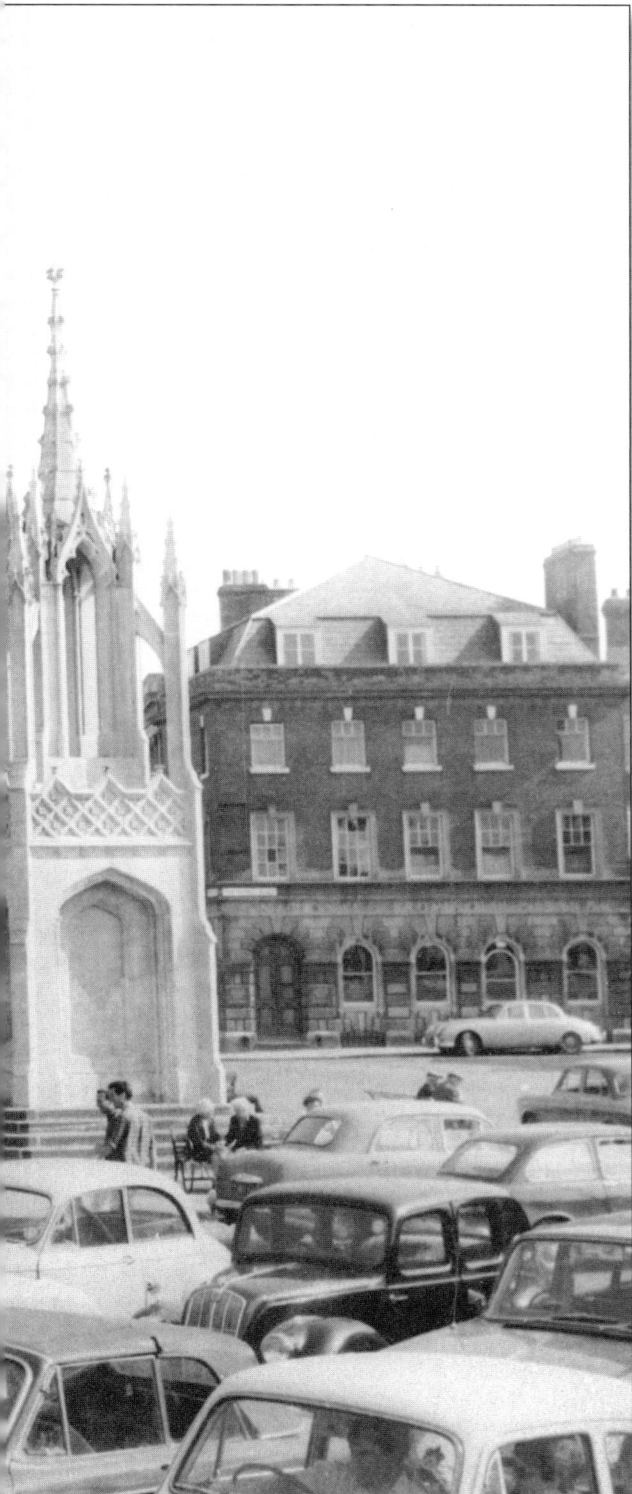

'a typically mixed Victorian affair, with a kind of Renaissance basin but Gothic shafts'.

Ansties' business premises (D28045, pages 26-27) extended the full length of Snuff Street. The ground floor was the leaf room. West Indian tobacco would come by canal to the factory from Bristol, which was processed into a variety of products. Popular lines were Otto de Rose snuff, sold at 2d a tin in the early years of the 20th century, and Farmer's Glory tobacco. Gold Flake cigarettes were 2d for ten during the First World War; they were the most popular line until 1961, when the company closed. It had ceased to be an independent family business when Imperial Tobacco took it over in 1944.

There is a variety of architectural styles and periods in the part of the Market Place which leads to Northgate Street — see D28071, pages 28-29. Opposite Anstie's, on the corner with Snuff Street, is the 1936 Co-op, built in fashionable Odeon style, now One Stop. The Black Swan next door at No 25 dates from the early 18th century. The date 1737 can be seen high up on the head of the cast iron rainwater pipe. The arched entrance to the old stables is well worth a look. The Pie Shop at No 24, now Hallmark Flooring, dates from 1840. Parnella House at No 23 is a fine 18th-century building with its elaborate front with six free-standing columns. The statue of Aesculapius, the Greek god of healing, shows that it was once a doctor's house. Further along is the 1912 Palace Cinema, which was very proud of its 'Western Electronic Mirrophonic sound system' in advertisements in the 1930s.

Below: Advertisements for E & W Anstie Ltd, Devizes and District Directory 1950

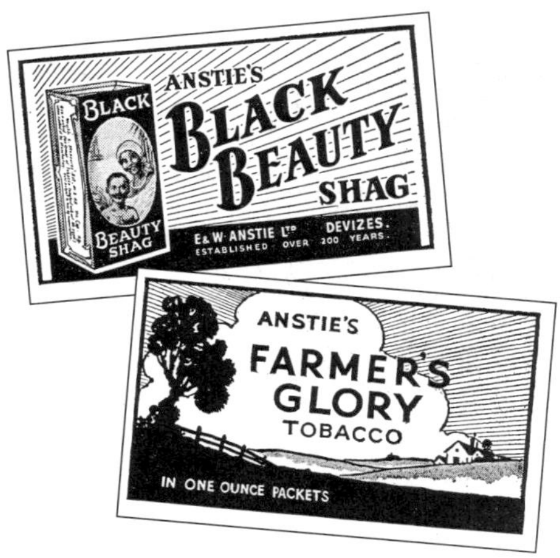

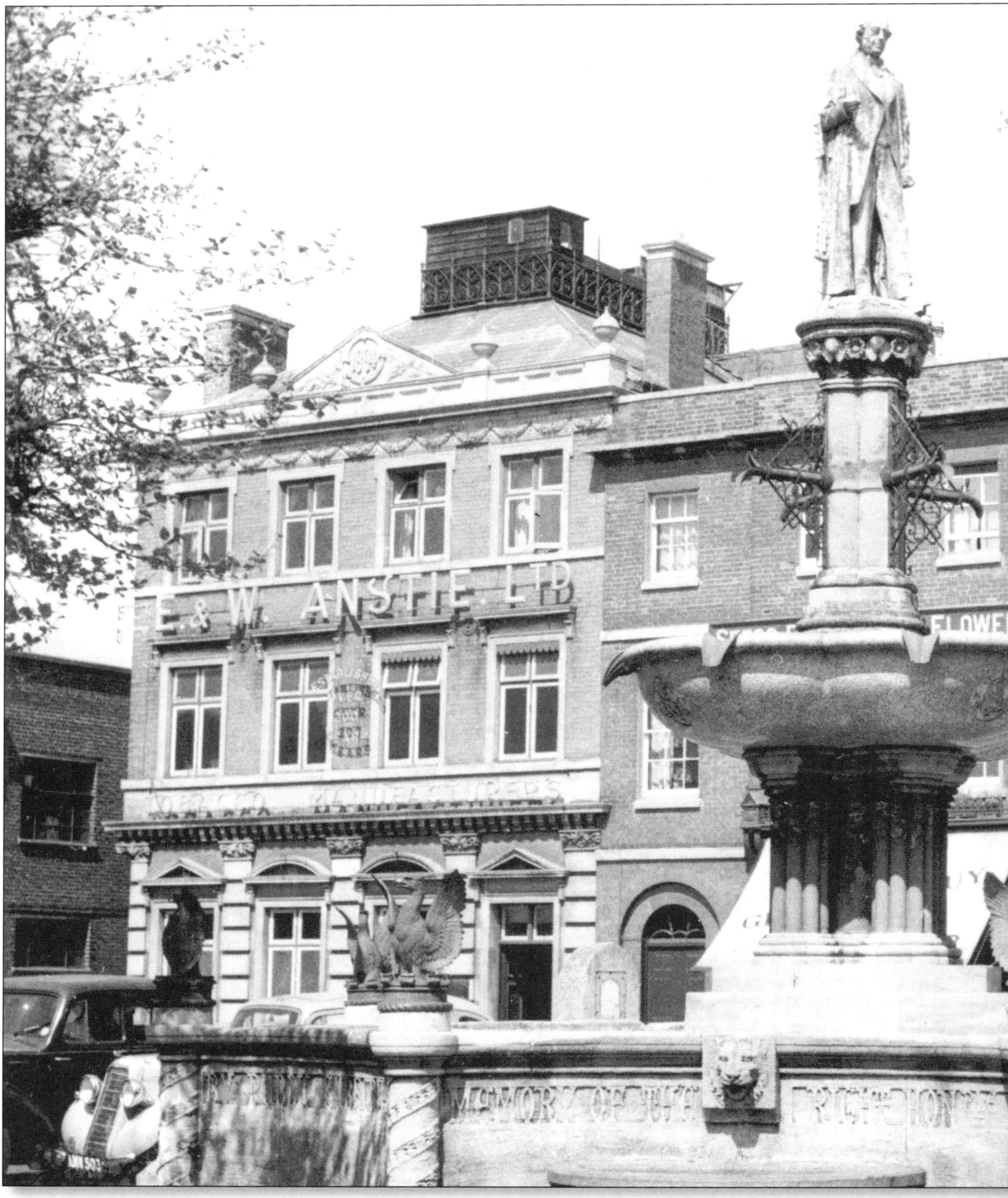
E & W. ANSTIE LTD

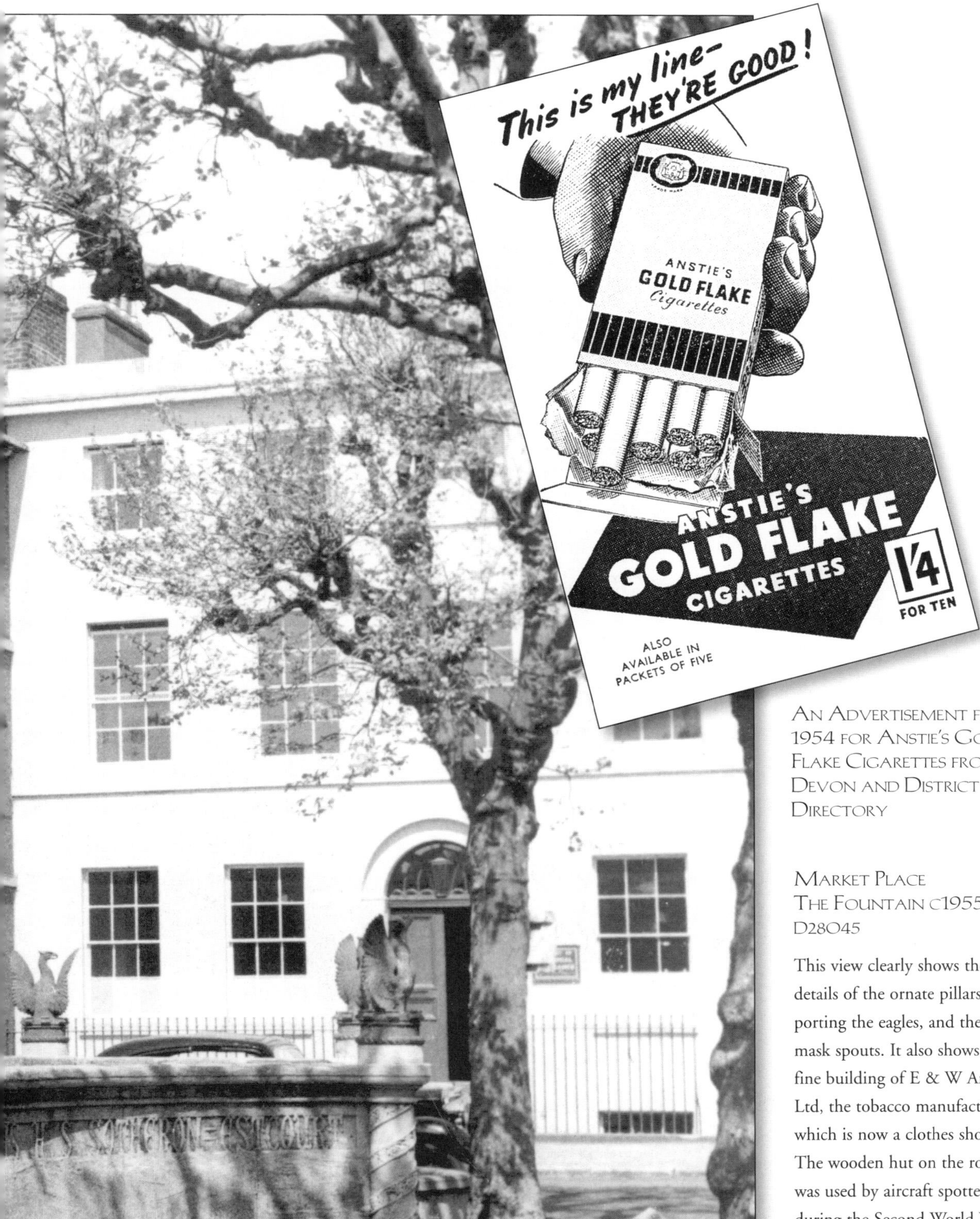

AN ADVERTISEMENT FROM 1954 FOR ANSTIE'S GOLD FLAKE CIGARETTES FROM DEVON AND DISTRICT DIRECTORY

MARKET PLACE
THE FOUNTAIN C1955
D28045

This view clearly shows the details of the ornate pillars supporting the eagles, and the lion mask spouts. It also shows the fine building of E & W Anstie Ltd, the tobacco manufacturers, which is now a clothes shop. The wooden hut on the roof was used by aircraft spotters during the Second World War.

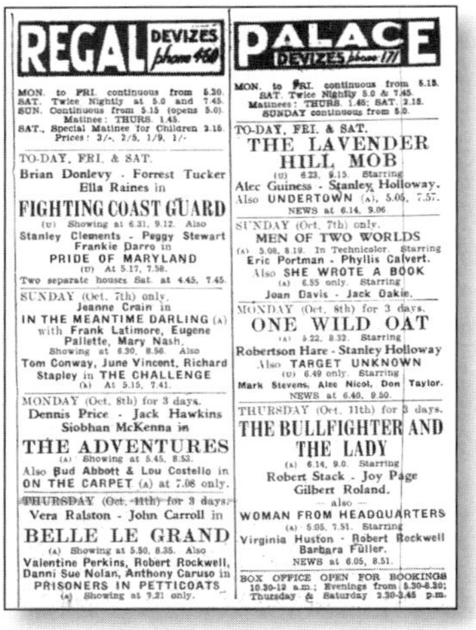

REGAL DEVIZES phone 460

MON. to FRI. continuous from 5.30.
SAT. Twice Nightly at 5.0 and 7.45.
SUN. Continuous from 5.15 (opens 5.0).
Matinee: THURS. 1.45.
SAT., Special Matinee for Children 2.15.
Prices: 3/-, 2/5, 1/9, 1/-

TO-DAY, FRI. & SAT.
Brian Donlevy - Forrest Tucker
Ella Raines in
FIGHTING COAST GUARD
(U) Showing at 6.31, 9.12. Also
Stanley Clements - Peggy Stewart
Frankie Darro in
PRIDE OF MARYLAND
(U) At 5.17, 7.58.
Two separate houses Sat. at 4.45, 7.45.

SUNDAY (Oct. 7th) only.
Jeanne Crain in
IN THE MEANTIME DARLING (A)
with Frank Latimore, Eugene
Pallette, Mary Nash.
Showing at 6.30, 8.56. Also
Tom Conway, June Vincent, Richard
Stapley in THE CHALLENGE
(A) At 5.15, 7.41.

MONDAY (Oct. 8th) for 3 days.
Dennis Price - Jack Hawkins
Siobhan McKenna in
THE ADVENTURES
(A) Showing at 5.45, 8.53.
Also Bud Abbott & Lou Costello in
ON THE CARPET (A) at 7.08 only.

THURSDAY (Oct. 11th) for 3 days.
Vera Ralston - John Carroll in
BELLE LE GRAND
(A) Showing at 5.50, 8.35. Also
Valentine Perkins, Robert Rockwell,
Danni Sue Nolan, Anthony Caruso in
PRISONERS IN PETTICOATS
(A) Showing at 7.21 only.

PALACE DEVIZES phone 171

MON. to FRI. continuous from 5.15.
SAT. Twice Nightly 5.0 & 7.45.
Matinees: THURS. 1.45; SAT. 2.15.
SUNDAY continuous from 5.0.

TO-DAY, FRI. & SAT.
THE LAVENDER
HILL MOB
(U) 6.23, 9.15. Starring
Alec Guiness - Stanley Holloway.
Also UNDERTOWN (A), 5.05, 7.57.
NEWS at 6.14, 9.06.

SUNDAY (Oct. 7th) only.
MEN OF TWO WORLDS
(A) 5.08, 8.19. In Technicolor. Starring
Eric Portman - Phyllis Calvert.
Also SHE WROTE A BOOK
(A) 6.55 only. Starring
Joan Davis - Jack Oakie.

MONDAY (Oct. 8th) for 3 days.
ONE WILD OAT
(A) 5.22, 8.32. Starring
Robertson Hare - Stanley Holloway
Also TARGET UNKNOWN
(U) 6.49 only. Starring
Mark Stevens, Alec Nicol, Don Taylor.
NEWS at 6.40, 9.50.

THURSDAY (Oct. 11th) for 3 days.
THE BULLFIGHTER AND
THE LADY
(A) 6.14, 9.0. Starring
Robert Stack - Joy Page
Gilbert Roland.
— also —
WOMAN FROM HEADQUARTERS
(A) 5.05, 7.51. Starring
Virginia Huston - Robert Rockwell
Barbara Fuller.
NEWS at 6.05, 8.51.

BOX OFFICE OPEN FOR BOOKINGS
10.30-12 a.m.; Evenings from 5.30-8.30;
Thursday & Saturday 2.30-3.45 p.m.

WHATS ON AT THE CINEMA OCTOBER 4 1951
FROM THE WILTSHIRE GAZETTE AND HERALD 4 OCTOBER 1951

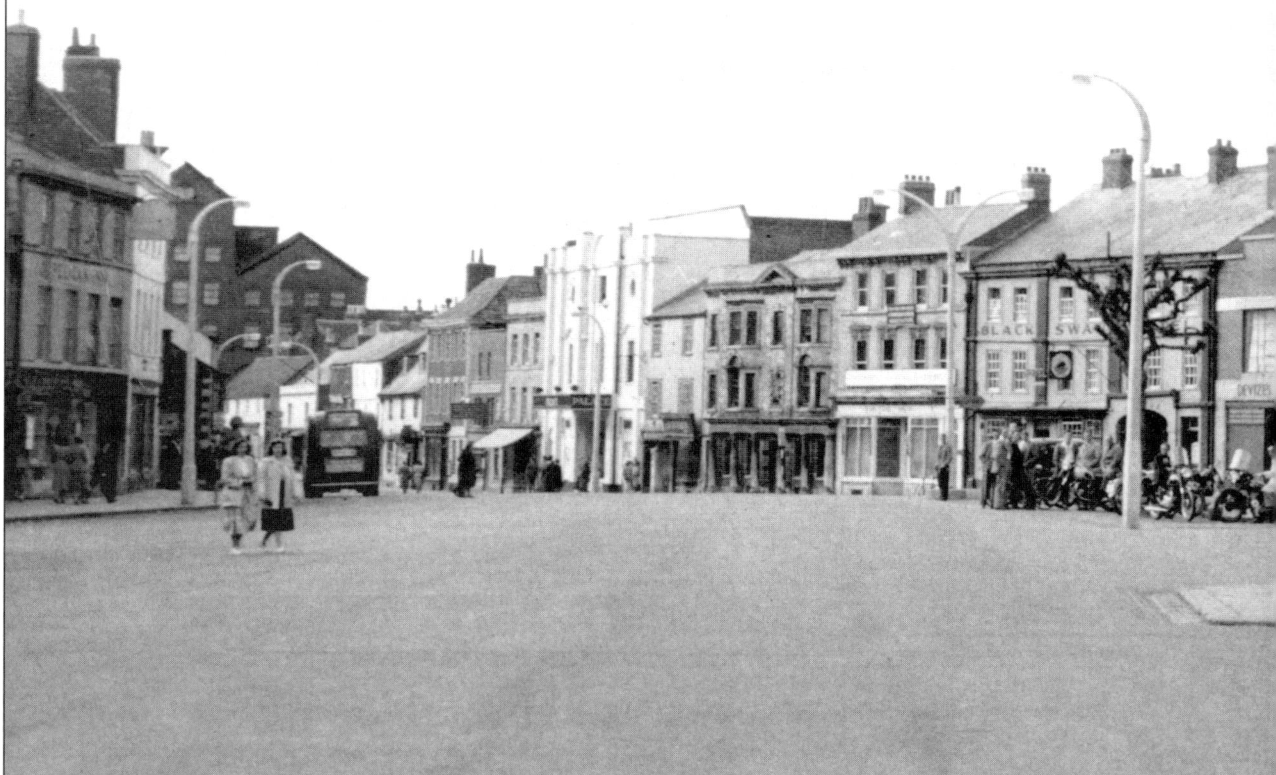

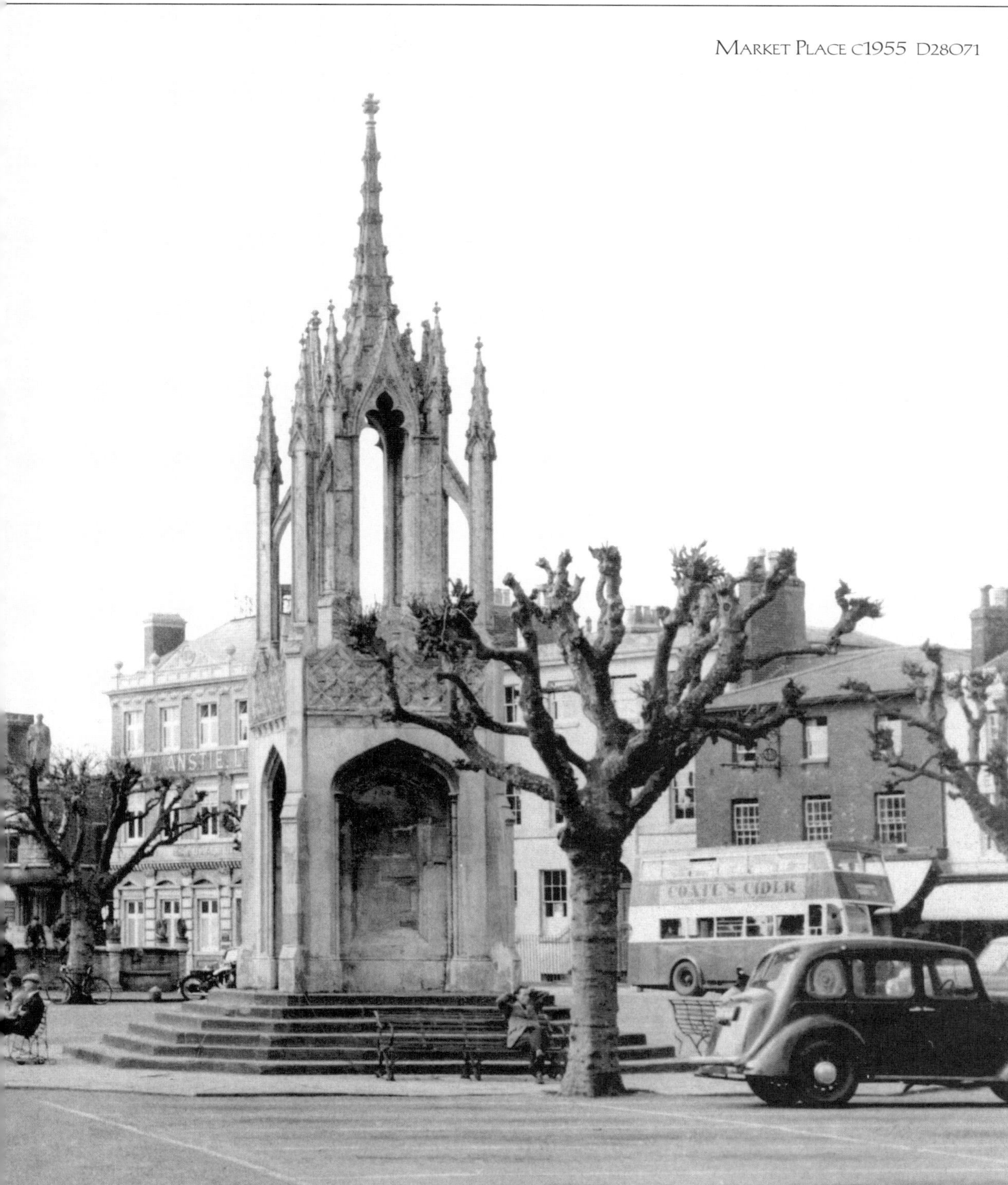

MARKET PLACE c1955 D28071

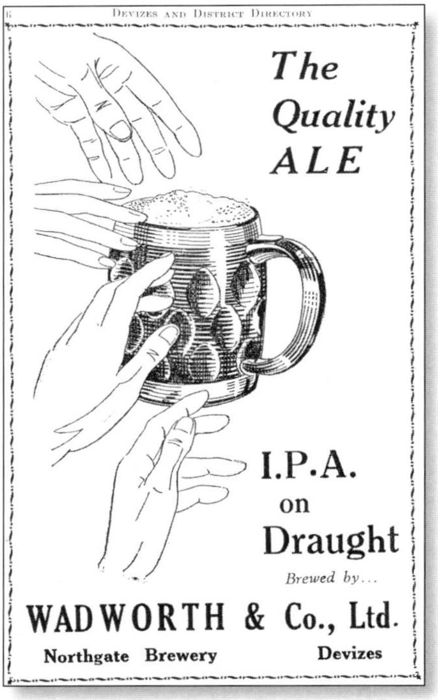

Above: An Advertisement for Wadworths

Below: Wadworths Brown Ale label, 1950s

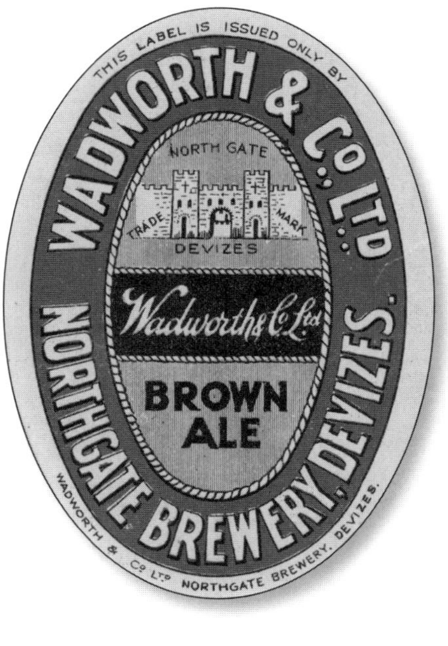

Northgate Brewery from Market Place c1955 D28053A

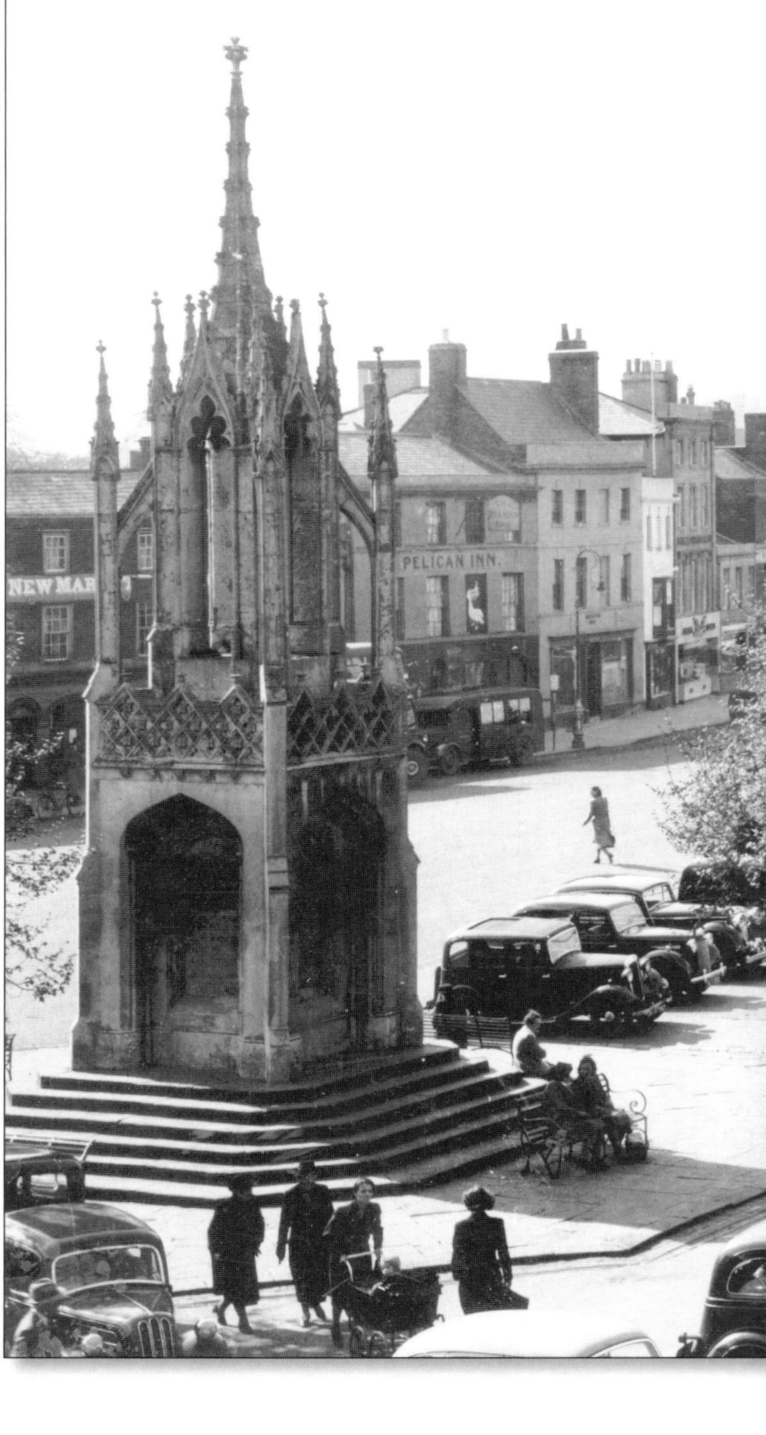

THE MARKET PLACE - WEST SIDE

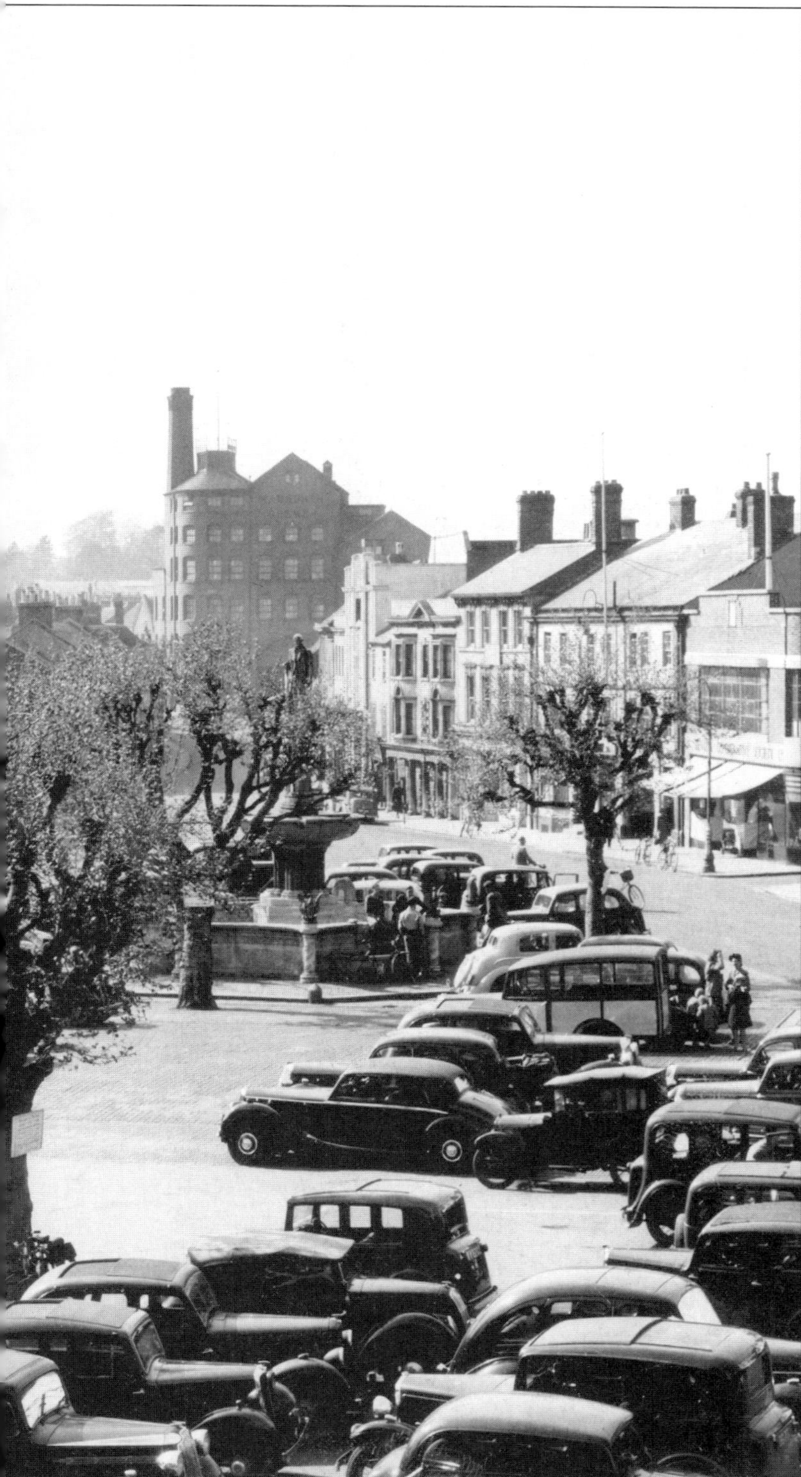

Brewing and malting have been taking place in Devizes since the mid 16th century. There were said to be ten maltsters and three brewers between 1620 and the mid 18th century. The tradition continues today with Wadworth & Co which has been brewing since 1875. Its founder, Henry Alfred Wadworth, started as manager of a small brewery at No 8 Long Street. Henry was in partnership with his brother-in-law, John Smith Bartholomew. The business is still owned and run by members of the Bartholomew family.

The Northgate Brewery is an imposing red brick building which dominates the western end of the Market Place. It was designed by Henry Alfred Wadworth in 1885 and built over the site of a small sweet water well. It has six storeys with a gabled centre, and a lower four-storey gabled section. A very tall square brick chimney rises from the yard above the roof line. The curved corner of the whole building softens the line of the road. A closer look at the brickwork shows attractive features at the gable ends where the cut brick copings give a bargeboard effect.

Wadworths is one of the town's biggest employers and even boasts its own cooper, Alastair Simms, one of only eight working in the country. He trained at Theakston's brewery in Yorkshire, and has been working in Devizes since 1995. Whilst metal casks are widely used, there is still a demand for beer 'from the wood'. Alastair concentrates on making new casks and re-coopering old ones, mainly kilderkins (which hold 18 gallons), firkins (9 gallons) and pins (4½ gallons). He has a fine display of old tools in his workshop, with strange names such as chiv, croze and jigger. Coopering today is a combination of machine and hand-made work.

CASK AND CORN

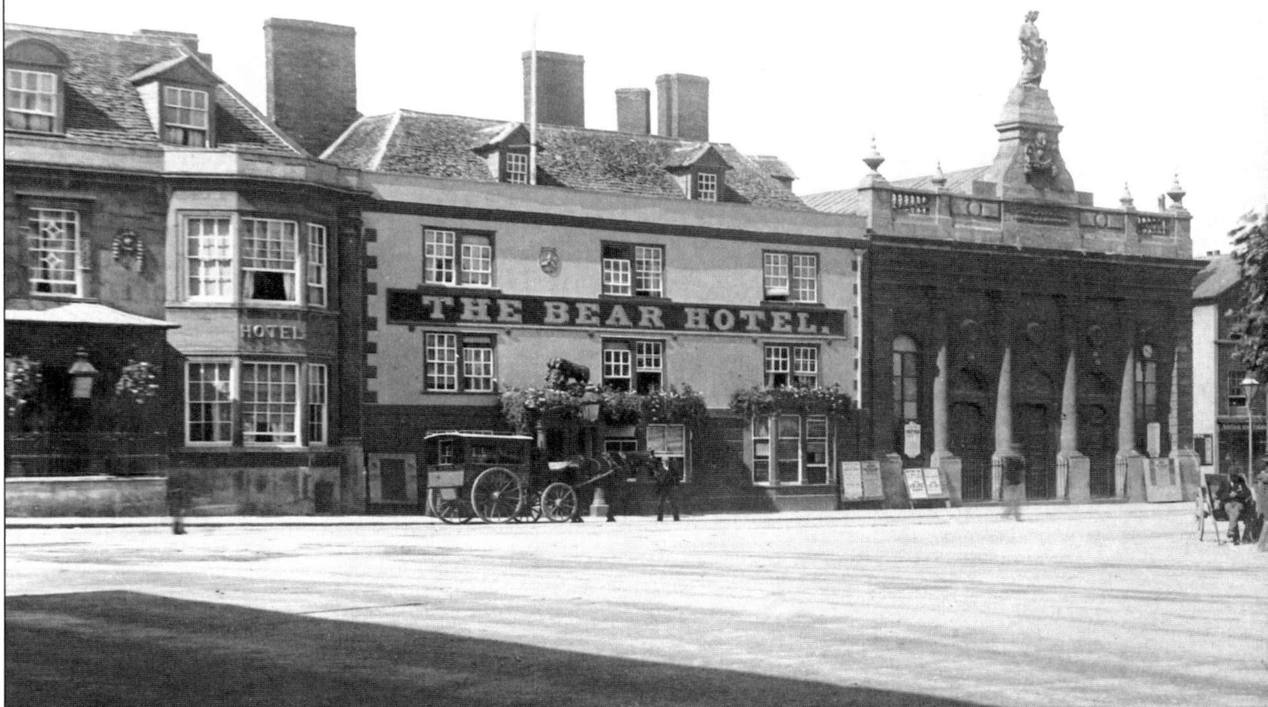

THE CORN EXCHANGE AND THE MARKET PLACE 1898 42301

Note the lovely horse and coach, which belongs to the Bear Hotel.

The old traditions also continue with the revival in 1974 of the shire horses and dray men. They are a familiar sight around the town each day, delivering casks to local public houses. The reputation of Wadworth's popular beers, such as 6X and Old Timer, is not just confined to the West Country. Their national reputation has increased along with diversification. In 1965 they bought up the premises called Wessex Wine in Long Street (see D28074 page 36) and the name of Edwin Giddings, a local wine merchant.

The Bear Hotel and the Corn Exchange represent two of the distinct characteristics of past and present life in the town: tourism and trade. They also connect town and country life and are a reminder of the agricultural life of the county.

The Bear Hotel, dating from at least the 16th century, stands in the south-west corner of the Market Place. It is two separate buildings, 'the left polite, the right homely', as Pevsner says. The left-hand side is late 18th-century, refaced in ashlar and given bay windows and fluted pilasters in about 1810. The pretty iron porch may be later. The right-hand building has an early 18th-century front to an earlier 16th- or 17th-century building. It is lower, and painted black and white. It has a deep porch with two Doric columns; a full-sized bear stands above, holding a large bunch of grapes. The hotel's name is painted across the front in 'bold Egyptian lettering'.

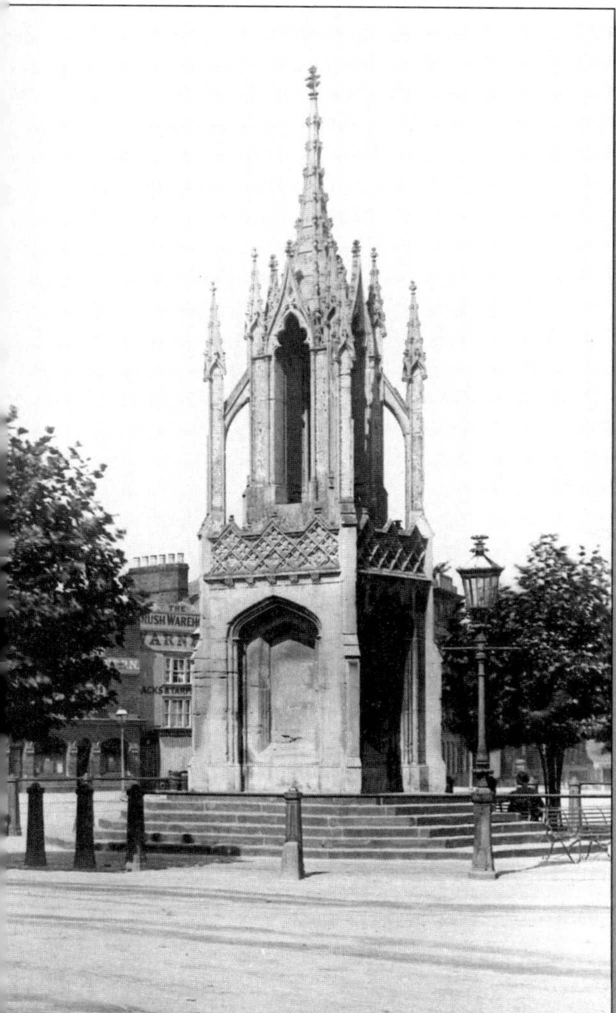

Inside on the main ground floor room there are Tuscan wood columns supporting the ceiling beams. In the far right-hand corner is an 18th-century staircase and a bow window. It is a delight for the modern visitor to move between the dark corners of the present bar areas to the light and airy splendour of the hotel lobby and restaurant.

Communications by road improved greatly after the Turnpike Acts. Devizes had its first turnpike road in 1706, and by 1753 there was a complete coaching route from Bath to London via Devizes. In 1790 there were two coaches daily, and the Bear was the most popular stopping-off place for travellers. It was also an important meeting place for locals. When George Whately was landlord in 1756, he started the Bear Club, which helped to provide education and apprenticeships for the poor boys of the town. Its attraction to members was also no doubt the jolly weekly get-togethers, including an annual dinner in August of turtle and venison.

In 1773, Thomas Lawrence became landlord — he and his wife had sixteen children, of whom three survived. He became famous for what might be termed today 'a successful marketing strategy': he erected 12ft posts at half-mile intervals across Salisbury Plain from Salisbury to Devizes 'to guide travellers in all weathers'. His youngest son, also Thomas, became a famous painter and President of the Royal Academy. The next landlord was William Halcombe; during his tenancy, between 1781 and 1801, there were twenty coaches stopping daily in Devizes. Some famous guests at this time were the Archduke and Archduchess of Austria in 1786 and King George III and Queen Charlotte in 1789.

In the 1966 film version of Thomas Hardy's 'Far from the Madding Crowd', starring Julie Christie, Alan Bates and Terence Stamp, the Corn Exchange and the Market Place were used as locations. Scenes where Bathsheba Everdene goes to sell corn and is treated with suspicion by the male farmers successfully conveyed the bustle, chatter and business. The trading of grain was similar to the present day Stock Exchange in its importance, as its price affected the local and national economy.

The Corn Exchange is a fine Bath stone building which looks earlier in date than 1857, when it was in fact built. Designed by a Leeds architect, W Hill, who won second prize in the competition to find a design, it was built on the site of the former Bear assembly rooms. Its main feature is the central statue of Ceres, the Roman goddess of tillage and corn, from which the word 'cereal' derives. The statue is set 'on a tall curved base with moulded capping and swag and cartouche ornament'. The building has been completely refurbished inside, and is an attractive venue for social events such as discos and concerts. It also holds regular antique fairs, which attract traders and visitors from Wiltshire and the surrounding counties.

Ordnance Survey Map

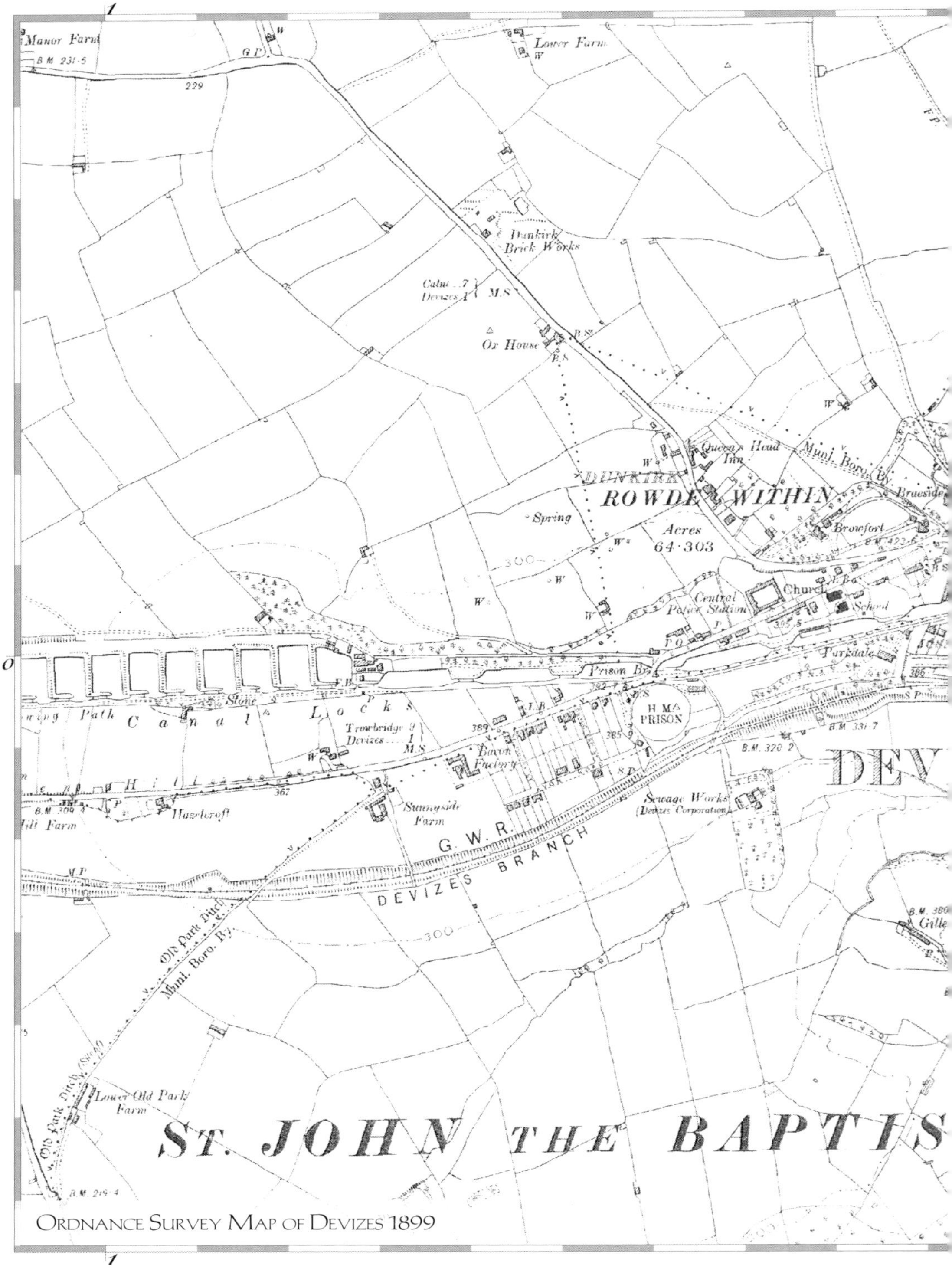

Ordnance Survey Map of Devizes 1899

DEVIZES

Ordnance Survey Map

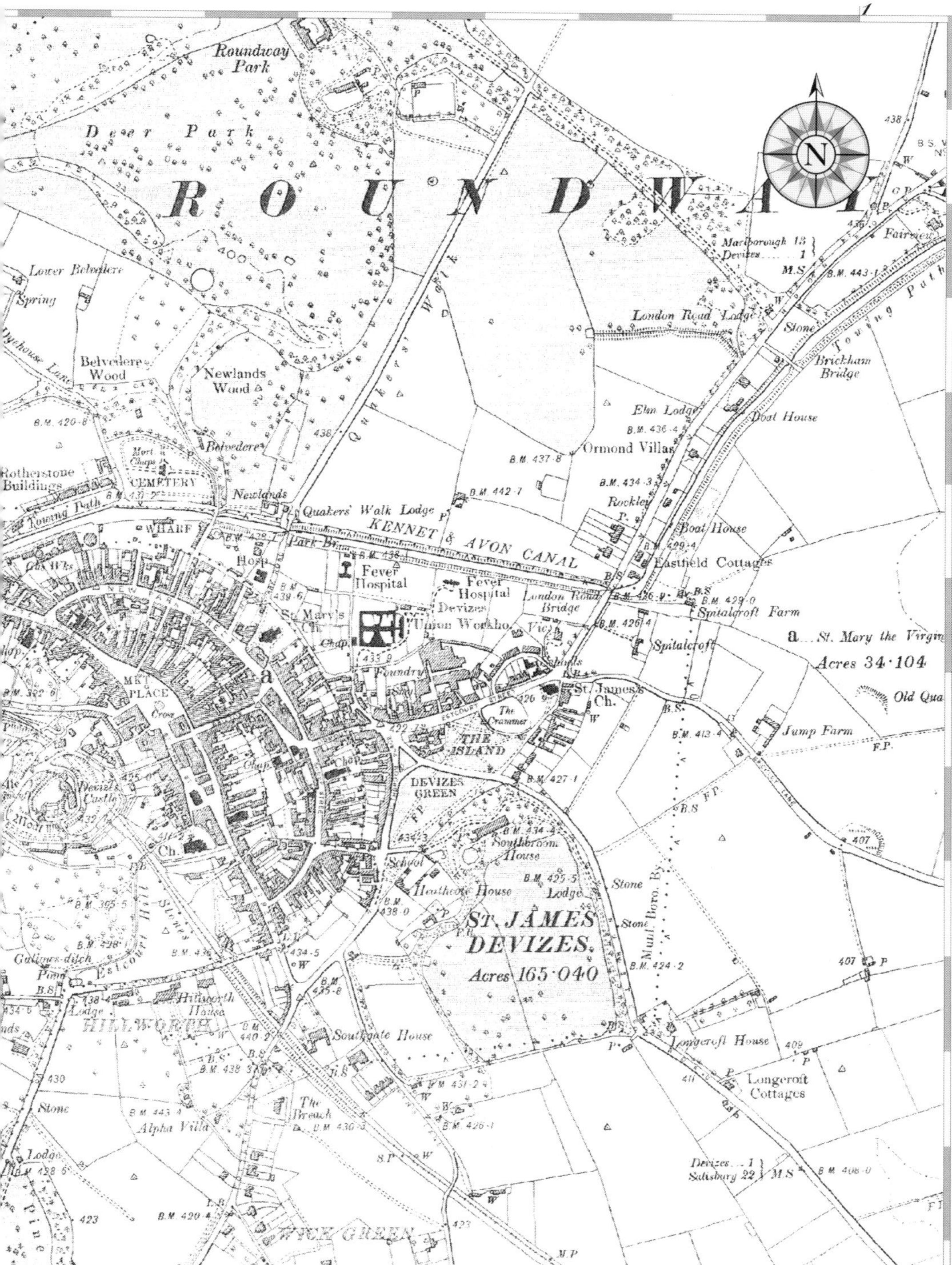

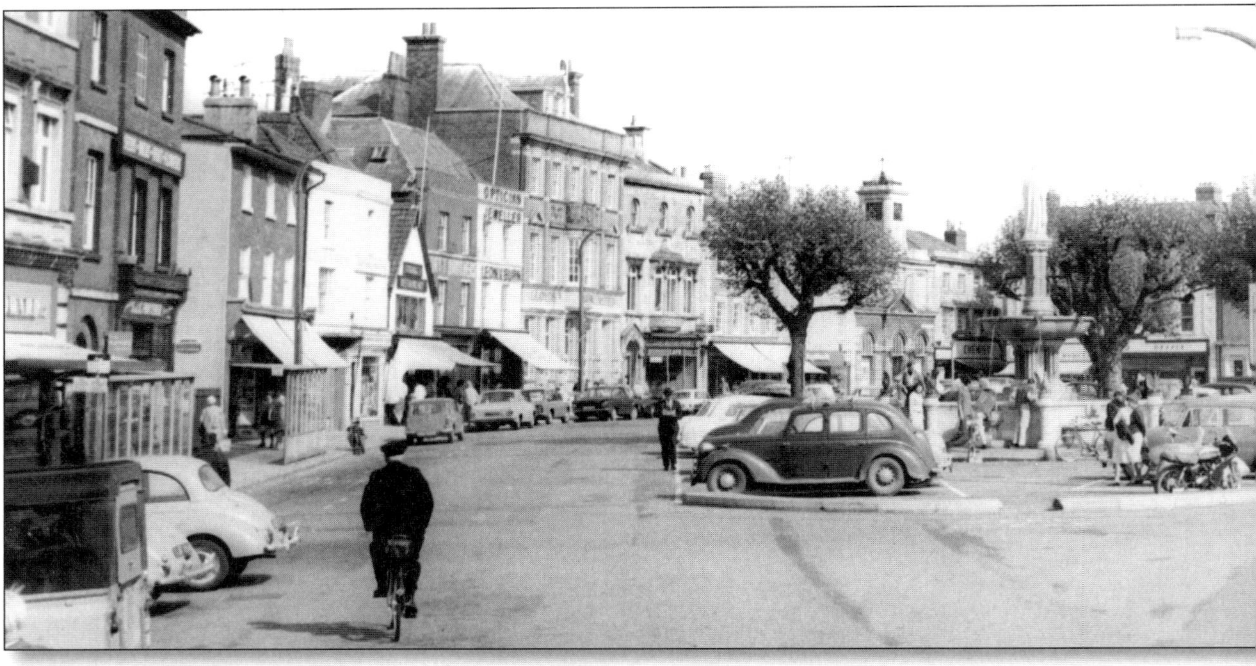

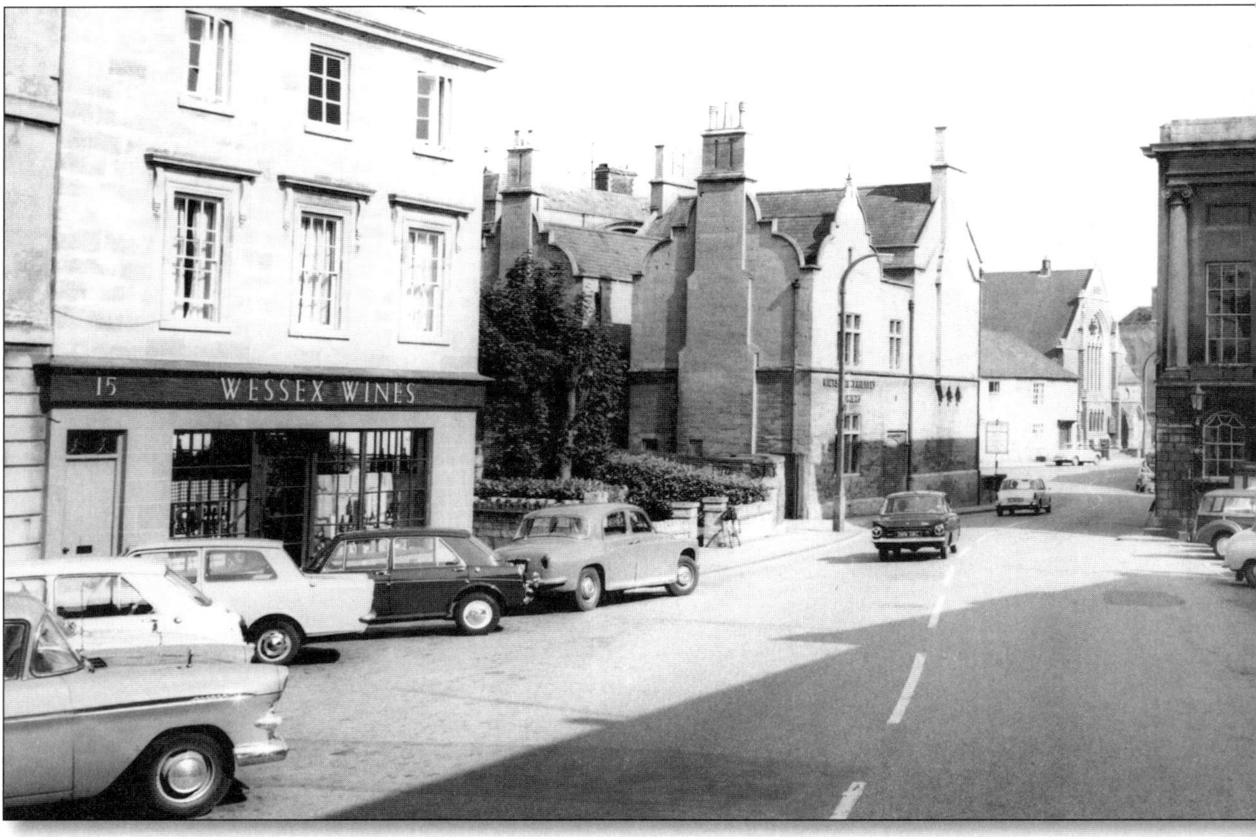
15
WESSEX WINES

THE TOWN HALL AND LONG STREET

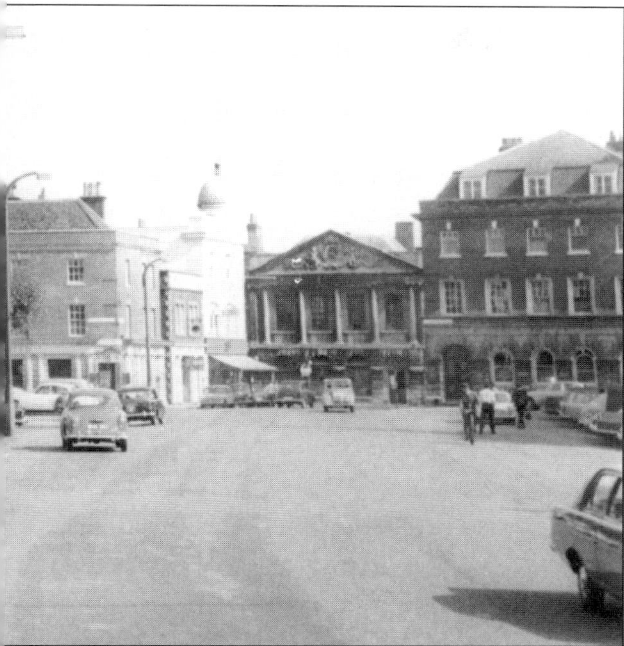

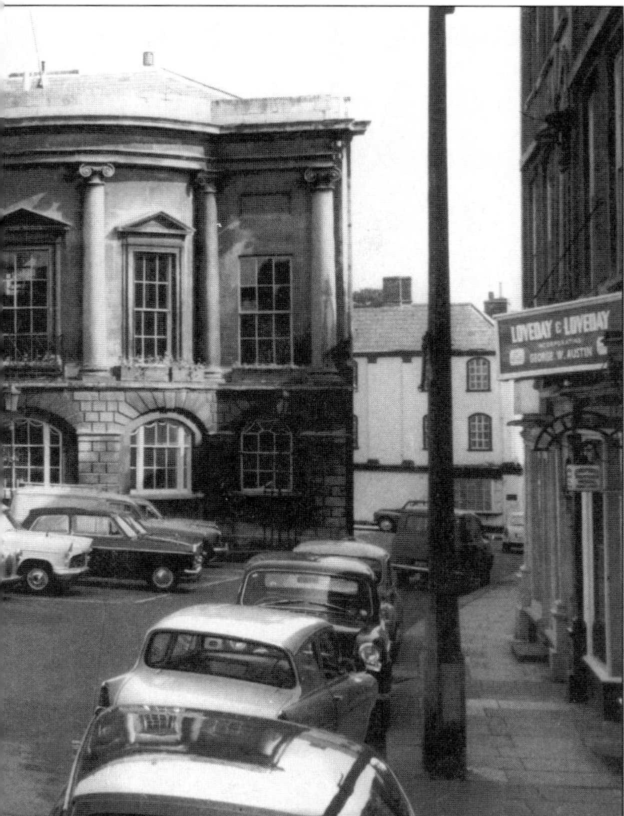

St John's Street leads from the Market Place into Long Street and out towards Salisbury. There are some interesting buildings in this part of the town; some of them reflect the civic and ecclesiastic history of the town, as well as the commercial and domestic. There are many well-preserved historic buildings, but there is sometimes an incongruous mix of styles.

On the way out of the Market Place into St John's Street we come to what is known as 'Boots Corner'. In 1912 a new building was erected at the corner of St John's Street and Wine Street to house a Boots store. The cash chemists moved a while ago, but they left a beautiful legacy in the form of the copper cupola (left and D28081A overleaf). The two sides of the upper storey are adorned with medallions. These have been beautifully restored, and show the heads of some of the important people in the town's history.

The new Town Hall (D28074) was designed by Thomas Baldwin, the designer of Bath's Guildhall, between 1806-8. It replaced the 17th-century Wool Hall which had fallen into disrepair. He incorporated some parts of the old building into the new. Pevsner describes it as 'a fine, elegant, accomplished little building'. The front has five bays and an ample bow at the centre; the ground floor is rusticated, with the windows in arched fields. There are handsome tall Ionic columns at first floor level. The building is rounded at the back (See 42306, page 40-41). The ground floor was originally open.

Top: MARKET PLACE c1960 D28082

The concrete lamps were hated by John Betjeman, who described them as 'sick serpents'. They do not marry well with the interesting skyline of the other buildings and monuments

Bottom: THE TOWN HALL c1960 D28074

This view down St John's Street shows the Town Hall. This building replaced the old one in Wine Street, which now houses the Cheltenham and Gloucester Building Society and Wine Street Gallery upstairs.

PIGEON PIES AND PENSIONS

The Town Hall was a popular meeting place; it was used as magistrates' court, a polling station and the venue for many social events. In her book 'Devizes, History & Guide', Lorna Haycock describes one mayor's feast in 1774: 'the guests consumed 77lbs of beef, 2 quarters of lamb, 1 sturgeon, 5 turbots, 4 cods, 4 sucking pigs, 4 turkeys, 12 ducks, 36 fowl, 4 geese, 20 tongues and 7 pigeon pies followed by rich fruit cakes, puddings and mince pies'. The wide stairway is decorated with a series of woodcarvings of the town's local history, and leads up to a fine assembly room with a musicians' gallery. The Adam-style plasterwork has been restored to its original glory; it is a delight to look up at the 'dolly mixture' colours. Visitors can view old photographs and a collection of gold and silver plate and borough regalia dating back to the 1600s.

At one time, the Town Hall boasted a 24-pound Russian cannon, brought back from the Crimean War, presented to the town in 1857, and displayed in front. It was removed during the Second World War for salvage, along with the railings.

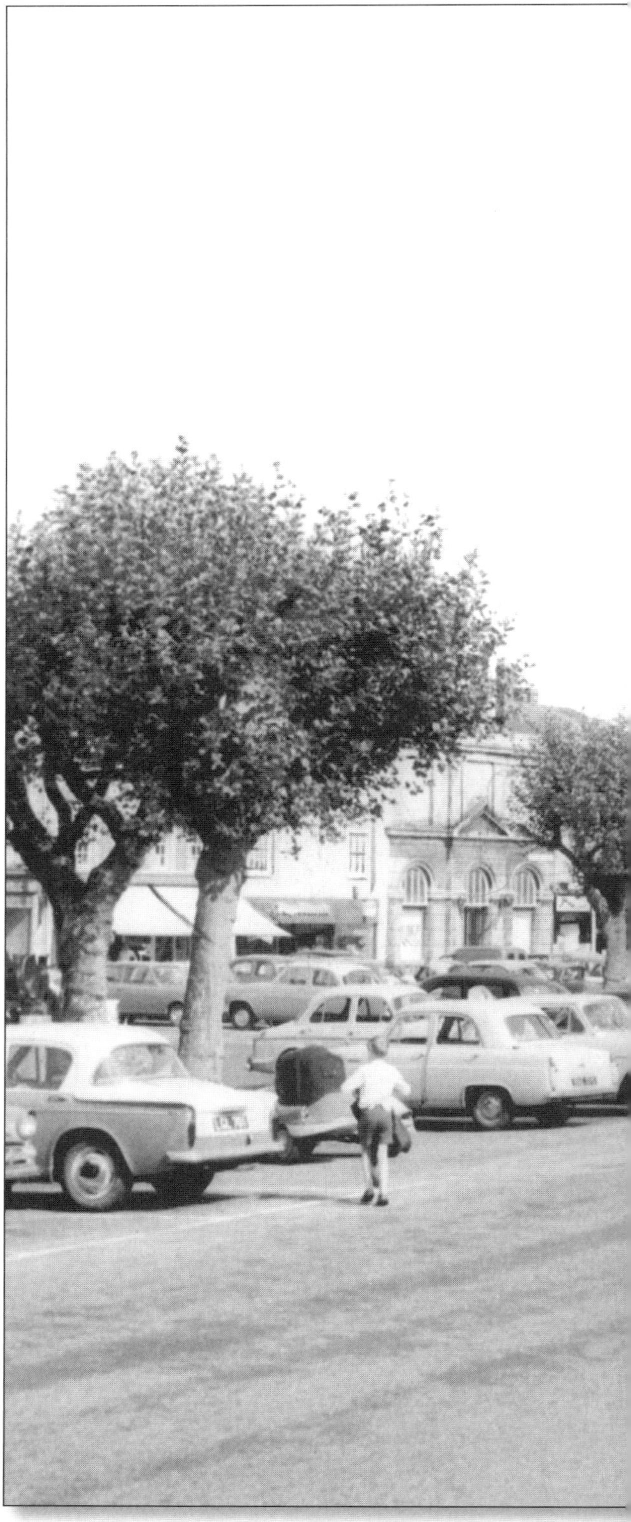

An Old Painting of Devizes Castle 1903 49901

This romanticised version of life at the Castle in medieval times can be seen in the Town Hall. It was painted by James Waylen, born in Devizes in 1810, the son of a clothier, Robert Waylen. He was first an engineer, then a painter, and also an historian; he wrote 'The Chronicles of Devizes' in 1839. As a contrast, there is a contemporary tapestry hanging on the stairway, which celebrates the 850th anniversary of the town's borough status.

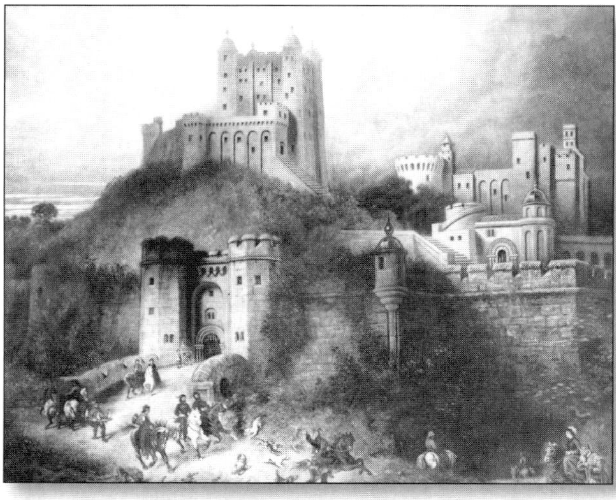

THE TOWN HALL AND LONG STREET

MARKET PLACE c1960 D28081

The old Town Hall (centre right) was built in 1752 on the site of the old Guildhall; the front is thought to have come from a demolished mansion. The lower part was originally open, and was used for the selling of eggs, butter and cheese. In 1836 it became the premises of the wine merchant William Cunnington, and extensive cellars run under the road and the buildings on the opposite side of the street.

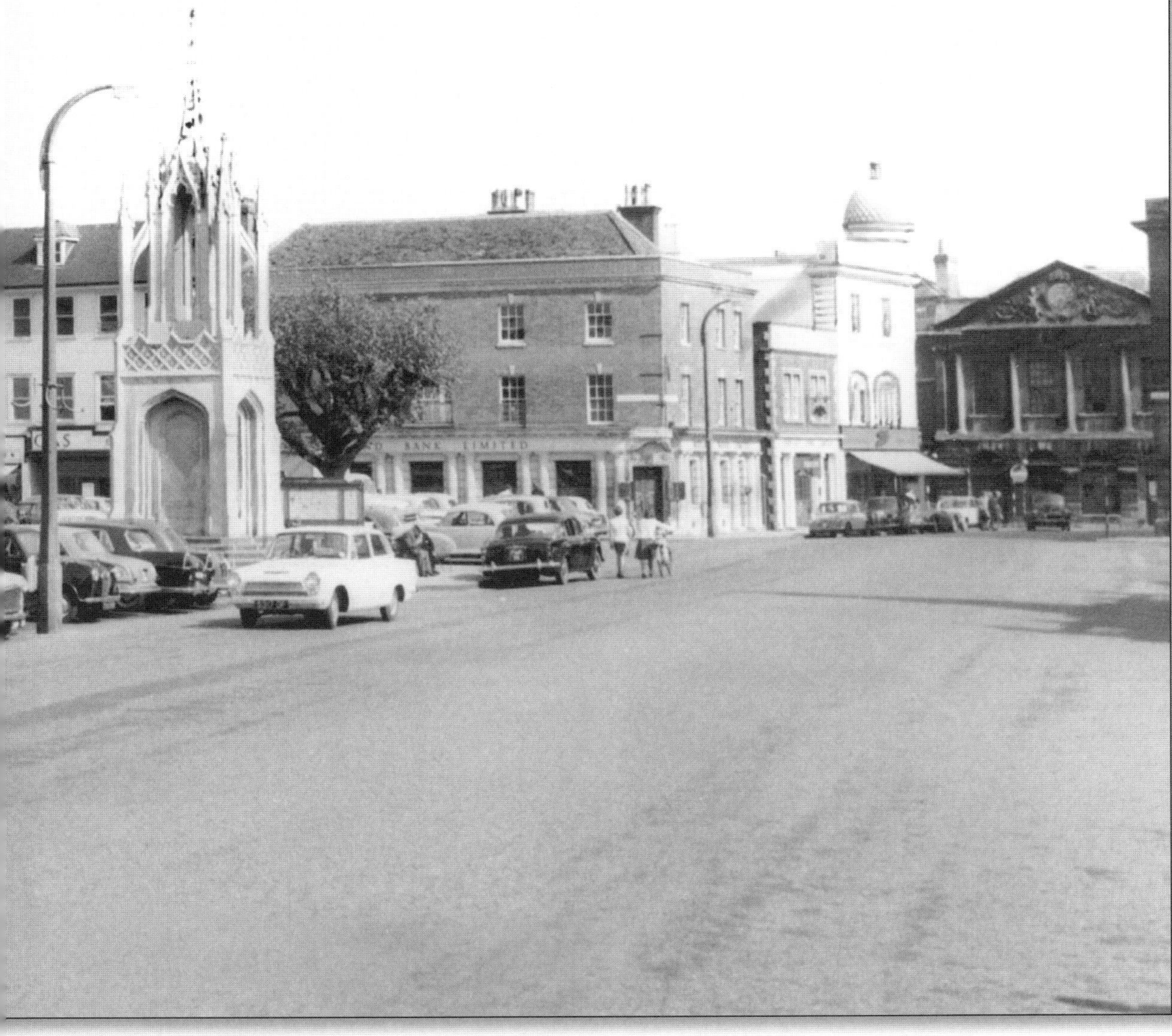

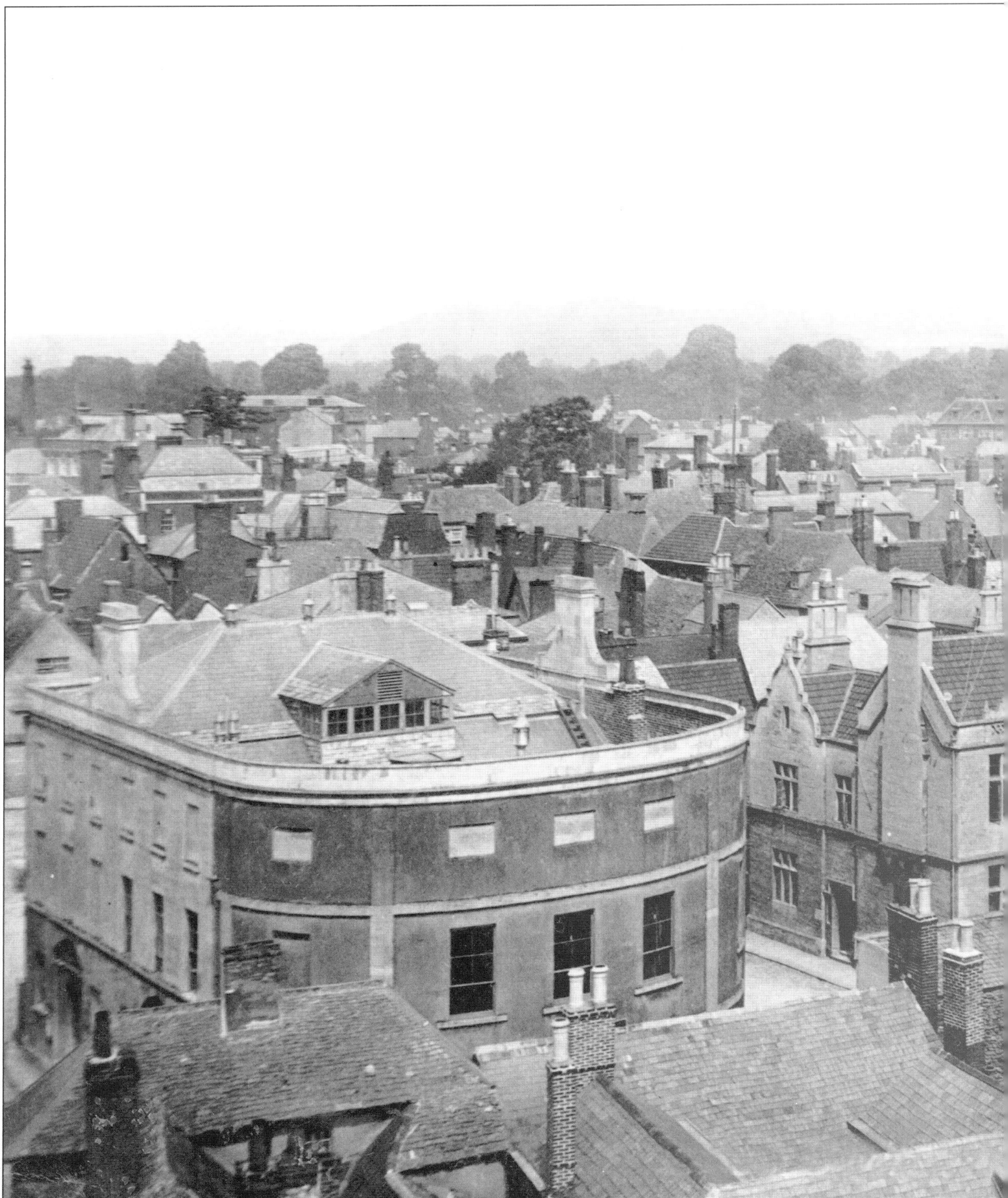

THE TOWN HALL AND LONG STREET

THE VIEW FROM ST JOHN'S CHURCH 1898 42306

This view across to St Mary's Church clearly shows a variety of architectural styles, including the unusual curved rear of the Town Hall on the left, the ornate gabled roof the Wiltshire Friendly Society building (centre), described by Pevsner as 'Victorian-Jacobean'; and the imposing Georgian grandeur of Greystone House to the right. Built in 1731, it is considered by Pevsner as 'rather a confused design'; the interior, however, is noteworthy for its fine staircase and plaster ceilings. Next door is The Elm Tree Inn, formerly The Salutation, and dating from the 17th century. The elm tree in front was removed in 1826.

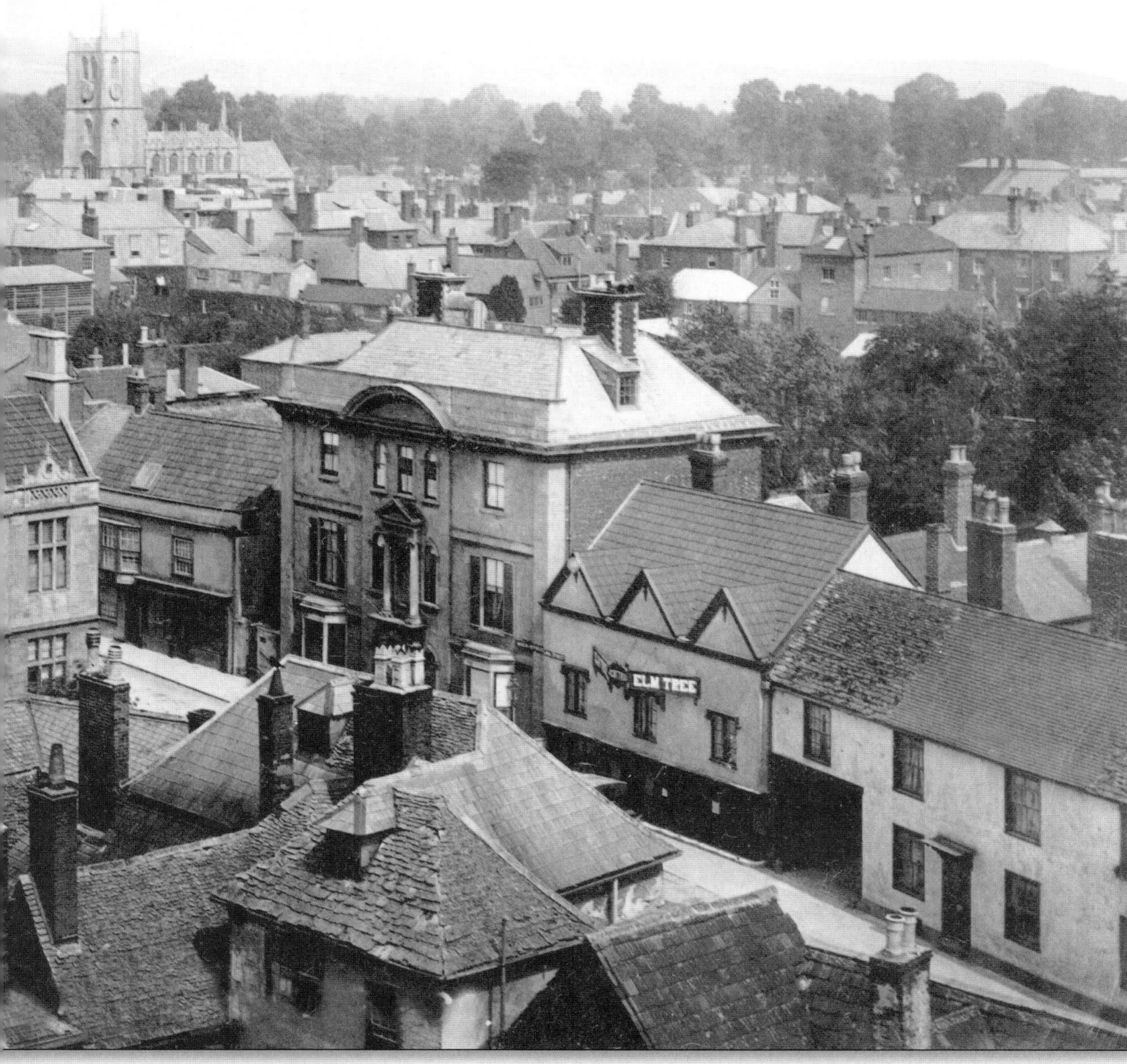

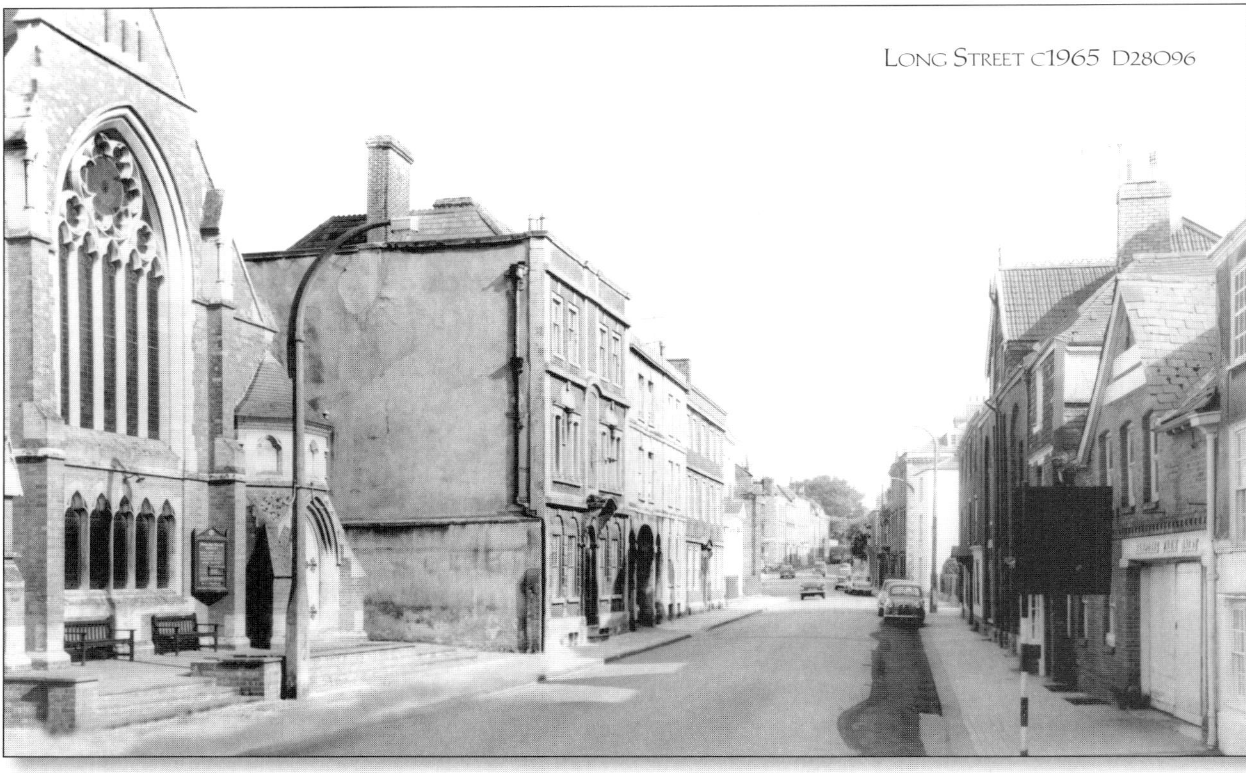

LONG STREET c1965 D28096

Next to St Andrew's Methodist and United Reformed Church (left of photograph) is No 8 Long Street, originally the home of Joseph Needham, a surgeon who was described in his obituary as 'perhaps the most celebrated man-midwife in the kingdom'. It is worth taking a closer look at some of the decorations on the front. On the right at Nos 48/49 is Hampton's Farm Dairy, now a hairdresser and mews cottages.

The Wiltshire Friendly Society (42306, 40-41) dominates the corner opposite the Town Hall where the High Street joins Long Street. Originally, Friendly Societies were set up in villages to help people when they were sick and to provide pensions to subscribers. They often met in public houses. The Wiltshire Friendly was established in 1828 by Thomas Sotheron Estcourt, and this building was erected in 1848. Accounts for the year 1873 show that sick pay was paid to 1,217 assurance members totalling £3,389 18s 4d, and in pensions, deaths and endowments £935 6s 0d was paid. The Society ceased in 1981. In 1987 the St John Ambulance Brigade took over the premises for their headquarters.

Long Street (D28096) leads out of town in the direction of Salisbury; it is lined with some magnificent Georgian-fronted houses — some façades hide earlier timber-framed structures. There is a mixture of private residences and businesses in the street now.

St John's Church can be approached from Long Street, or along St John's Street through into St John's Walk. Photograph D28095 shows the approach from St John's Street. The timber-framed, stuccoed and colourwashed houses, Nos 1-3, are 16th- to 17th-century buildings altered in the 18th century. On the other side is the Liberal Club, which has recently been restored. This was the home of William Cunnington, a local wine merchant and also a famed geologist. Some of his collection of fossils can be found in the Museum.

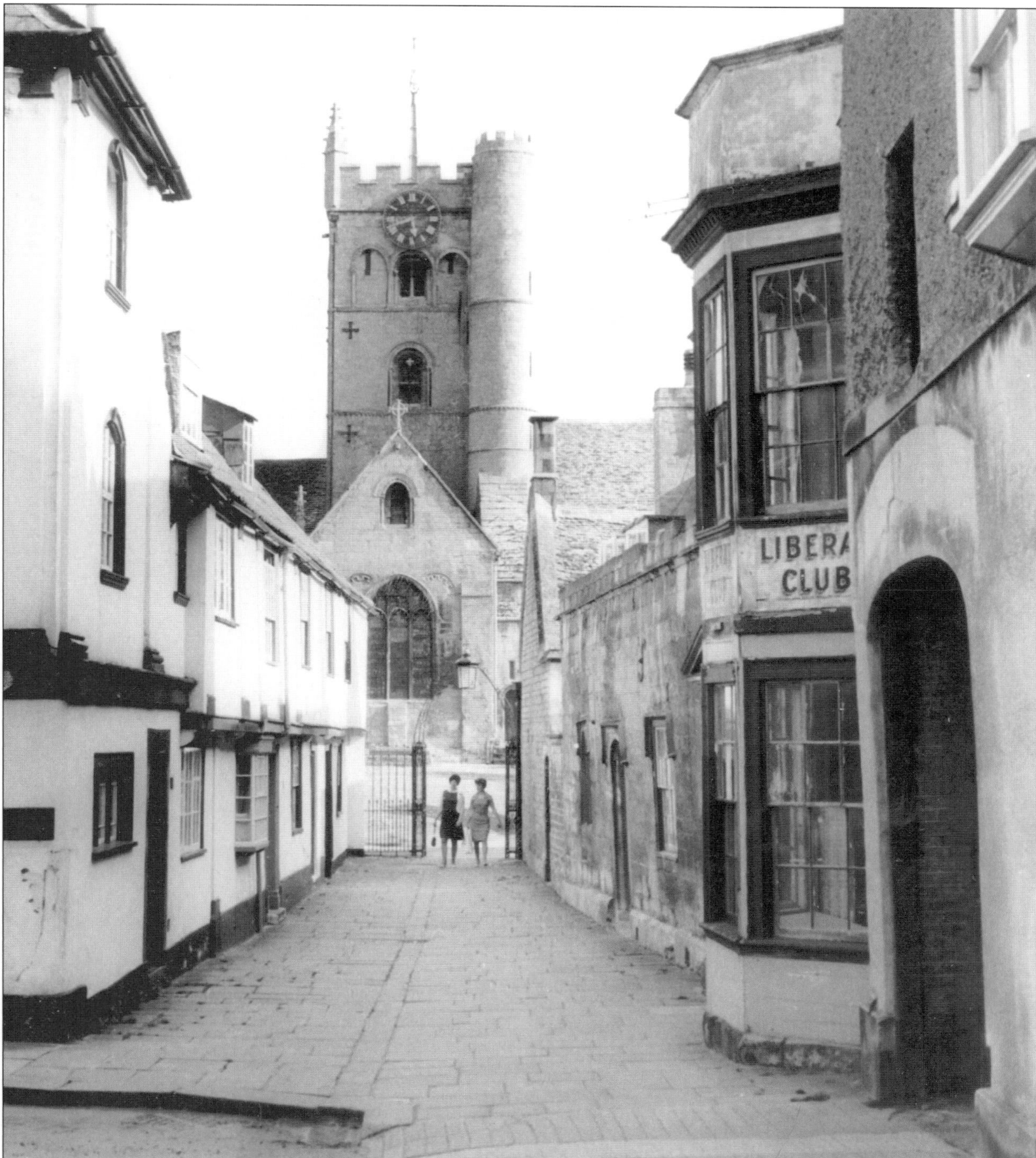

ST JOHN'S WALK C1965 D28095

BEETHOVEN, BREECHES AND BUNS

The Brittox is one of the main shopping streets in Devizes. It was called 'La Bretasche' in the 14th century, and was probably a path forming part of the defence stockade of the castle. The types of shops have changed little over the last hundred years. You can still buy shoes, bread and cakes, medicines, toys and stationery, as locals could do a hundred years ago; although they could also buy a piano and sheet music, have a saddle made and a chair upholstered within this one street.

The department store of Charles Sloper stood where Boots and Woolworths now have their businesses. The family firm developed and expanded over a century to keep up with local demands and with changing tastes.

At the end of the Brittox runs Maryport Street (D28098, page 46-47), which is now a one-way street. The motorist has to take care along this street, as it is a busy thoroughfare for pedestrians who shop here and along Sidmouth Street. Apart from two major supermarkets, and some of the usual chain retail shops, there is a high percentage of independent traders here. The newsagents E F Duck and Son, Bucklands Footwear and H J Johnson, jewellers, are long-established businesses.

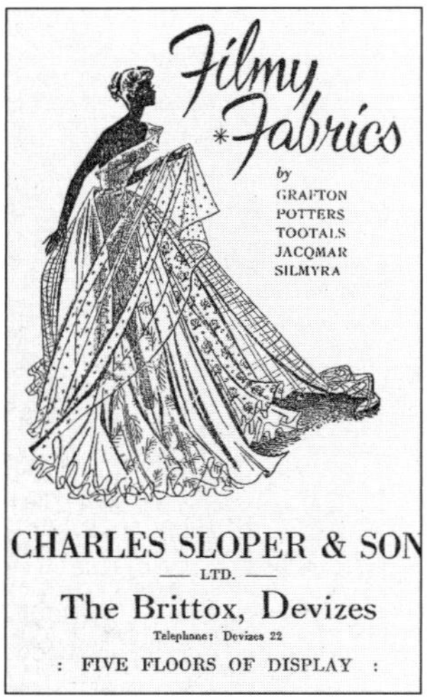

ADVERTISEMENT FOR CHARLES SLOPER & SON, FROM THE DEVIZES AND DISTRICT DIRECTORY 1961

Handel House, on the corner of Sheep Street and Sidmouth Street, is a beautiful building with Greek Doric columns dividing the shop windows from each other. It has been recently restored and decorated with some of its original features, which reflect the music business of Ezra Price. He established a music shop in the Brittox in 1847, and moved into New Road House in 1872. A former coachman and a self-taught piano tuner, he named the premises Handel House in 1880 when he painted panels with composers' names. He expanded his empire throughout the south-west, still naming each shop Handel House. The building continued as a music shop under the management of G H Oliver until 1971. It was a carpet shop until 1986, when it became Devizes Books.

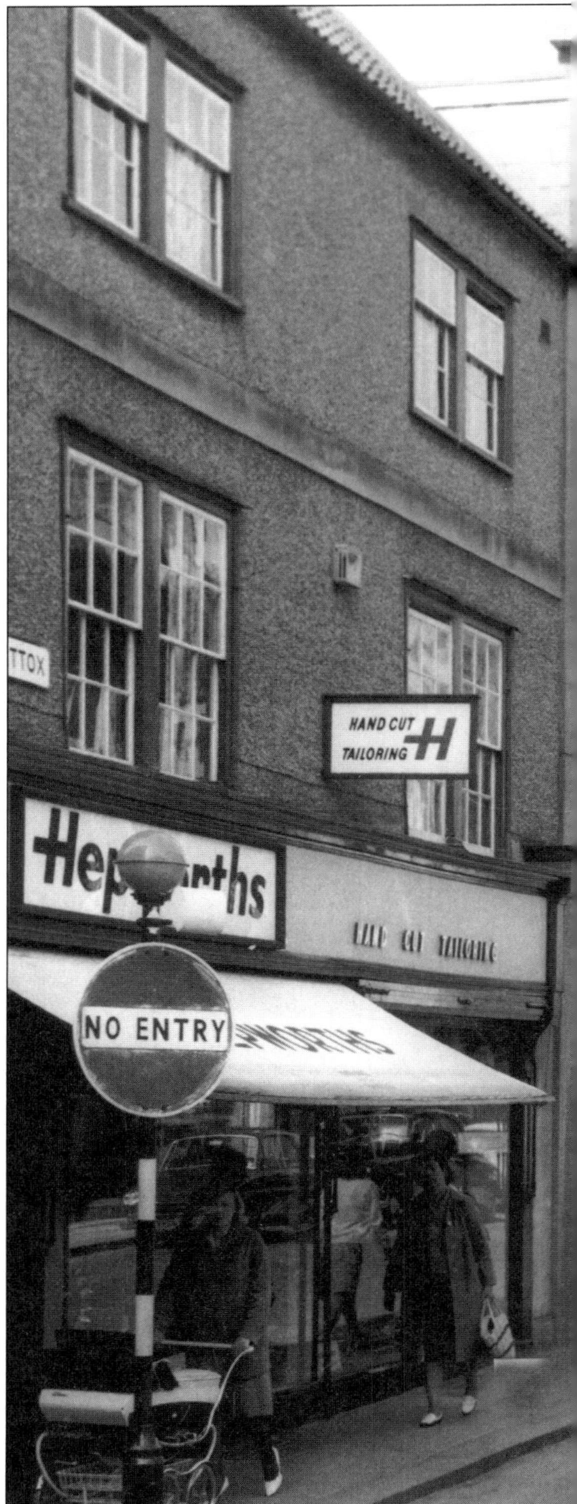

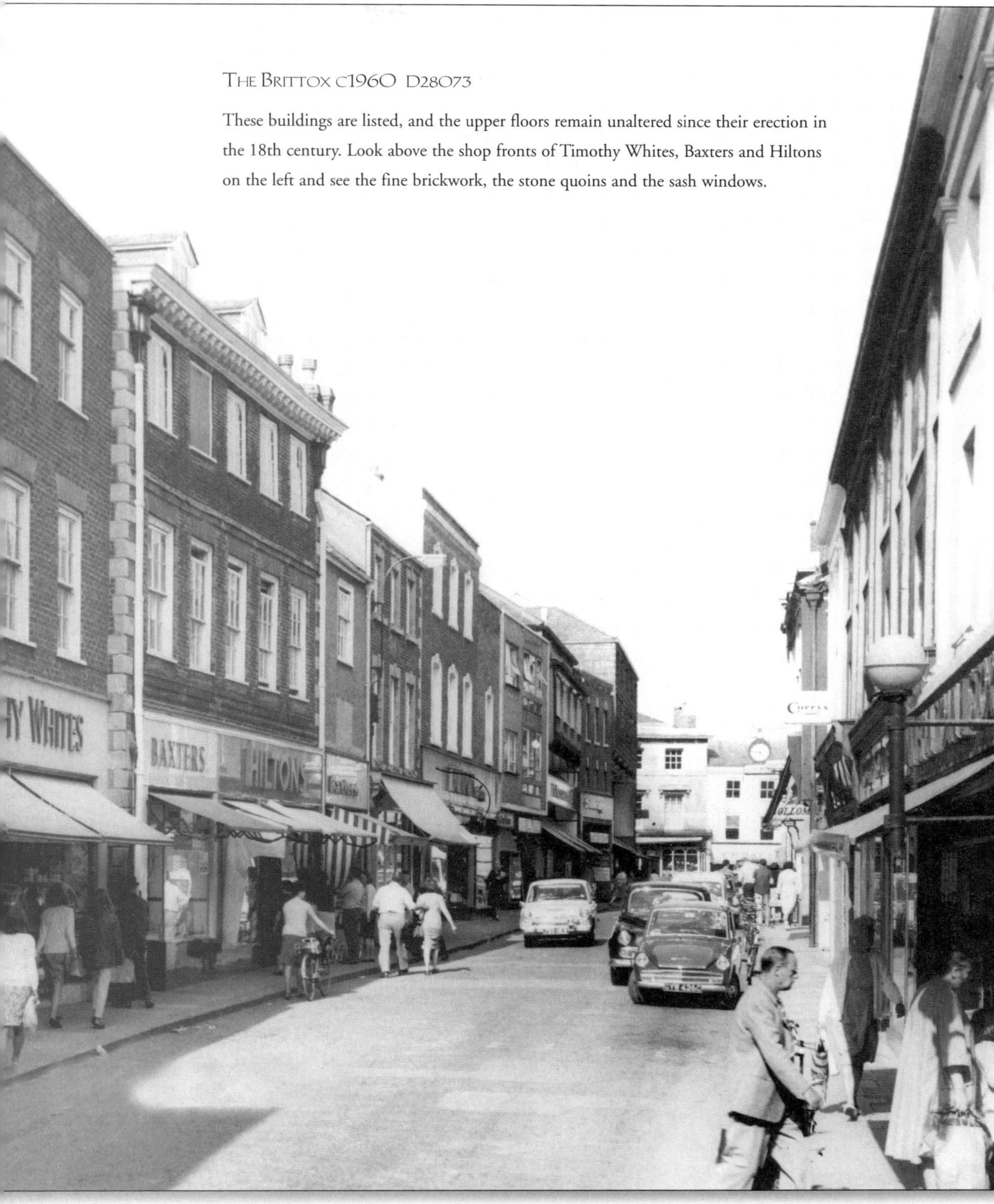

THE BRITTOX c1960 D28073

These buildings are listed, and the upper floors remain unaltered since their erection in the 18th century. Look above the shop fronts of Timothy Whites, Baxters and Hiltons on the left and see the fine brickwork, the stone quoins and the sash windows.

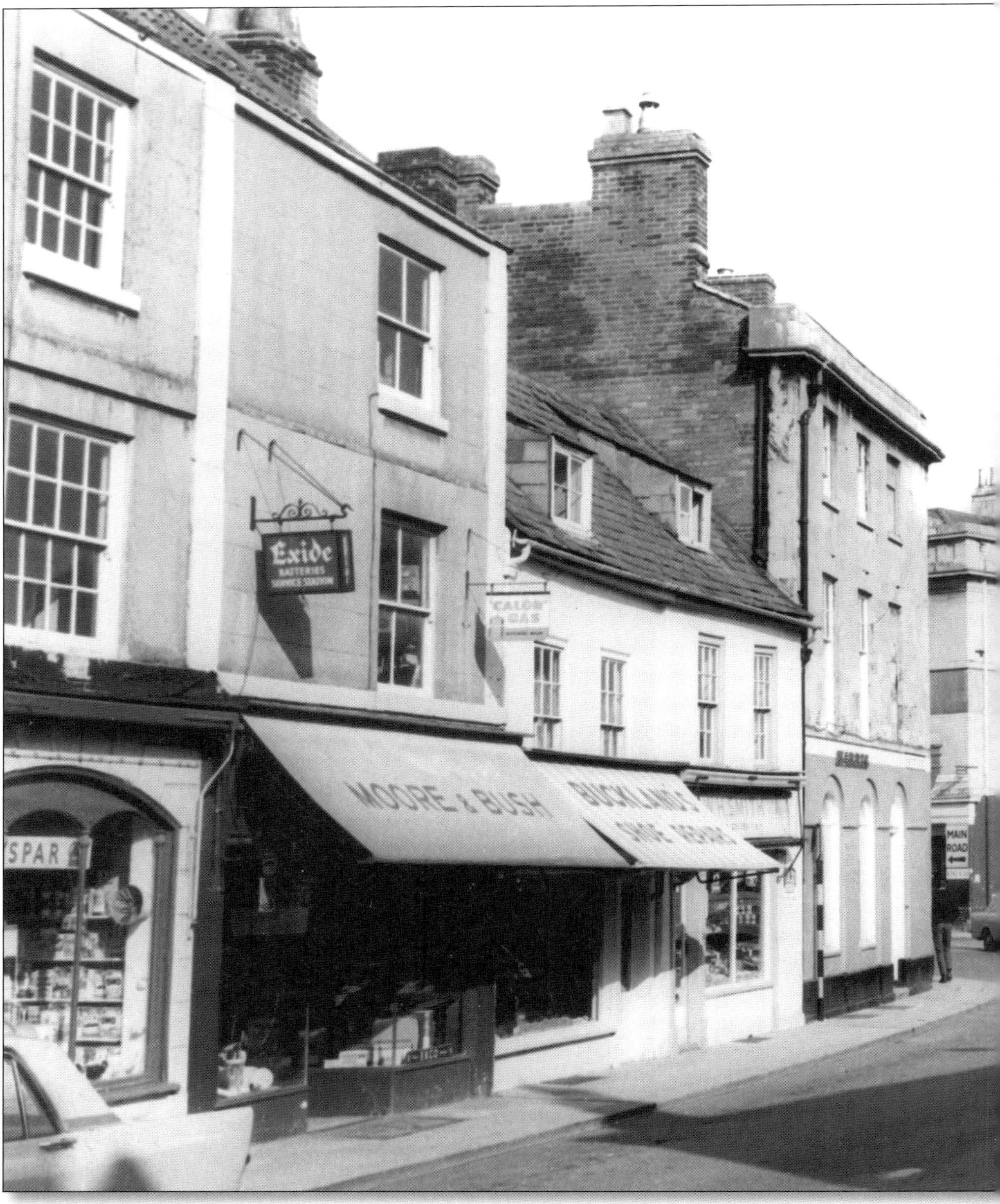
Exide
BATTERIES
SERVICE STATION
CALOR
GAS
SPAR
MOORE & BUSH
BUCKLAND'S
SHOE REPAIRS
MAIN
ROAD

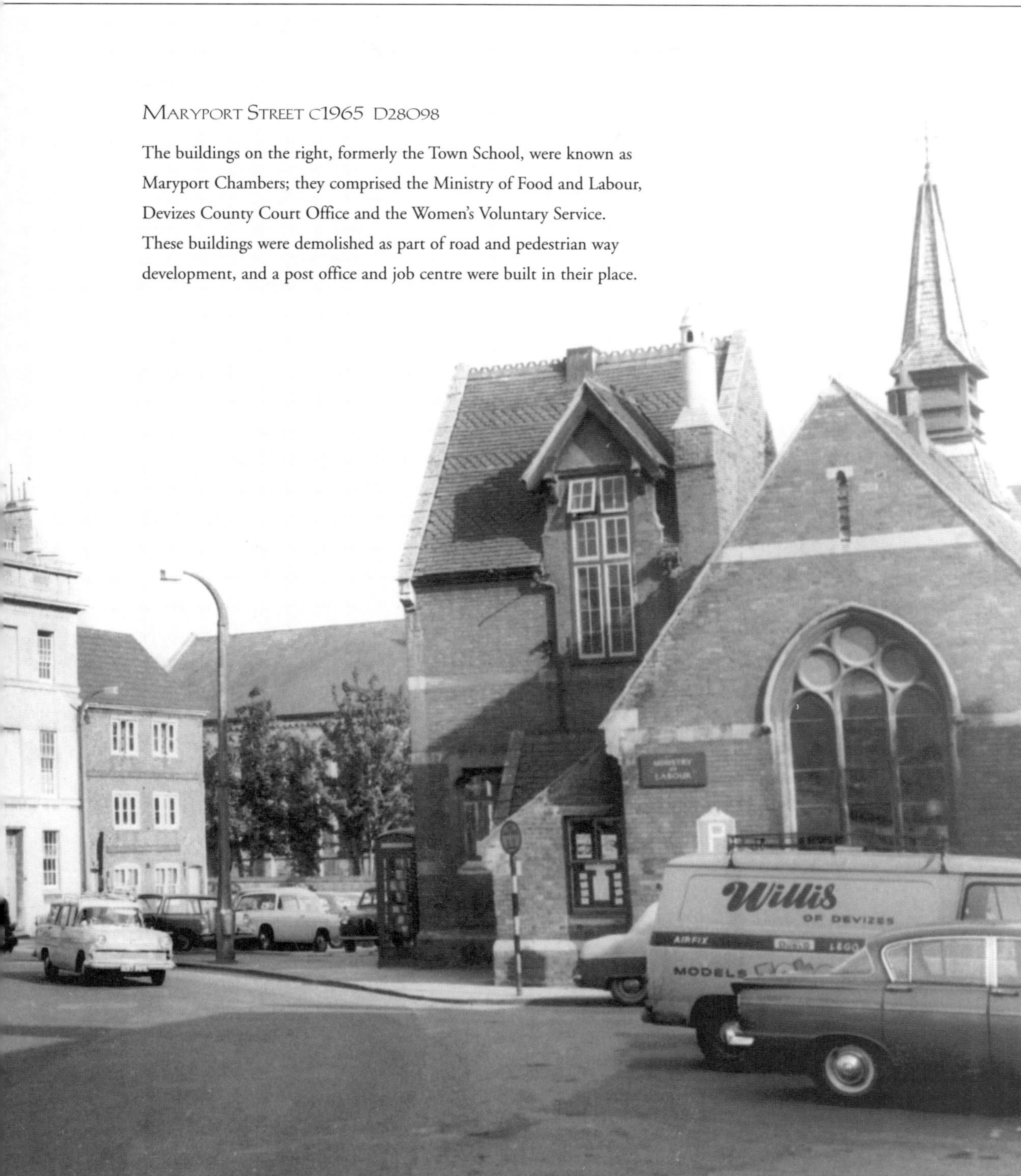

MARYPORT STREET C1965 D28098

The buildings on the right, formerly the Town School, were known as Maryport Chambers; they comprised the Ministry of Food and Labour, Devizes County Court Office and the Women's Voluntary Service. These buildings were demolished as part of road and pedestrian way development, and a post office and job centre were built in their place.

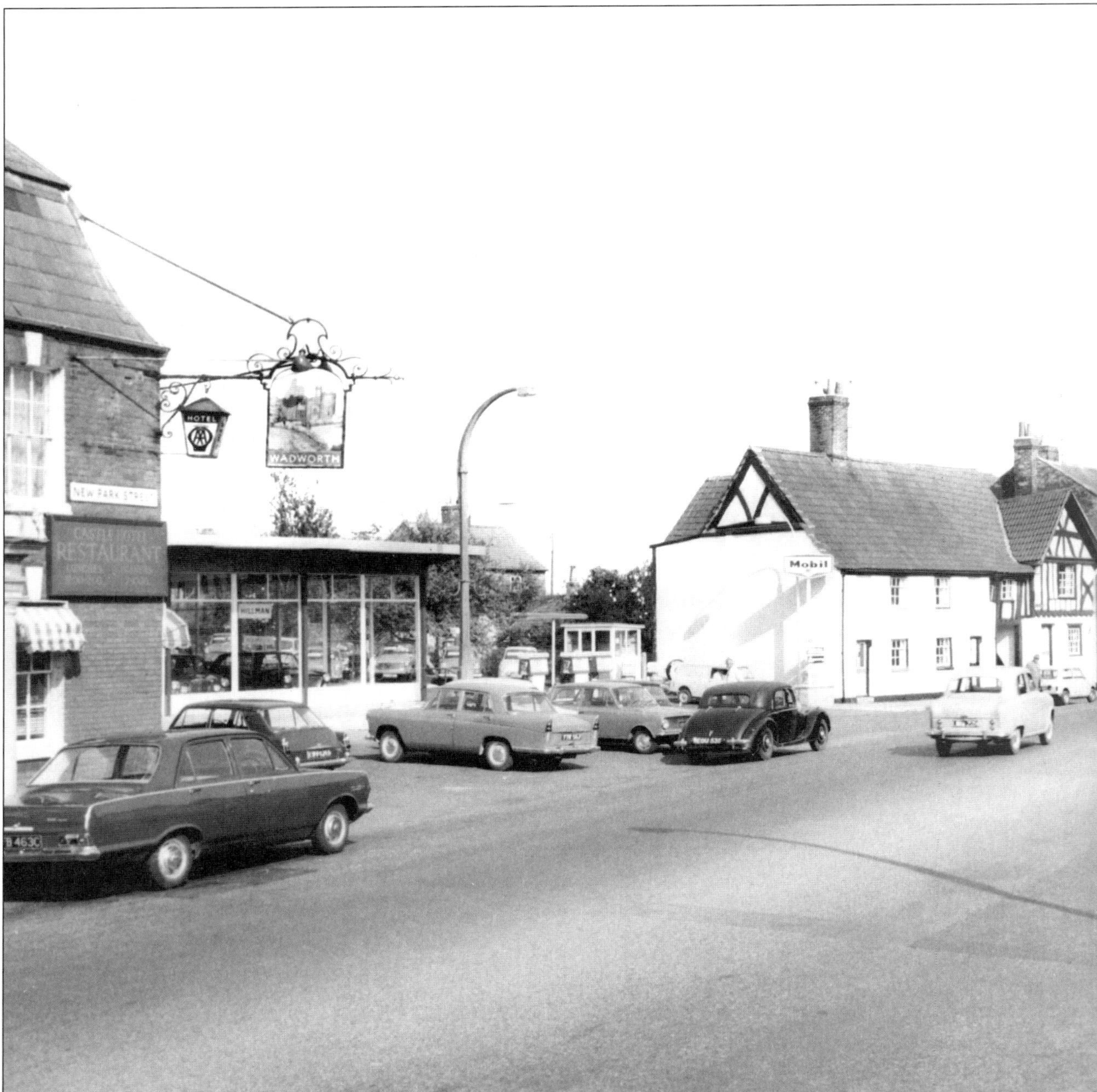

NEW PARK STREET c1965 D28090

Road developments have altered this view. Chantry Court forms the corner of the new ring road which cuts through the garage of Wadham Stringer on the left; this was formerly the Regal Cinema, which closed in 1959.

THE BRITTOX TO ESTCOURT STREET

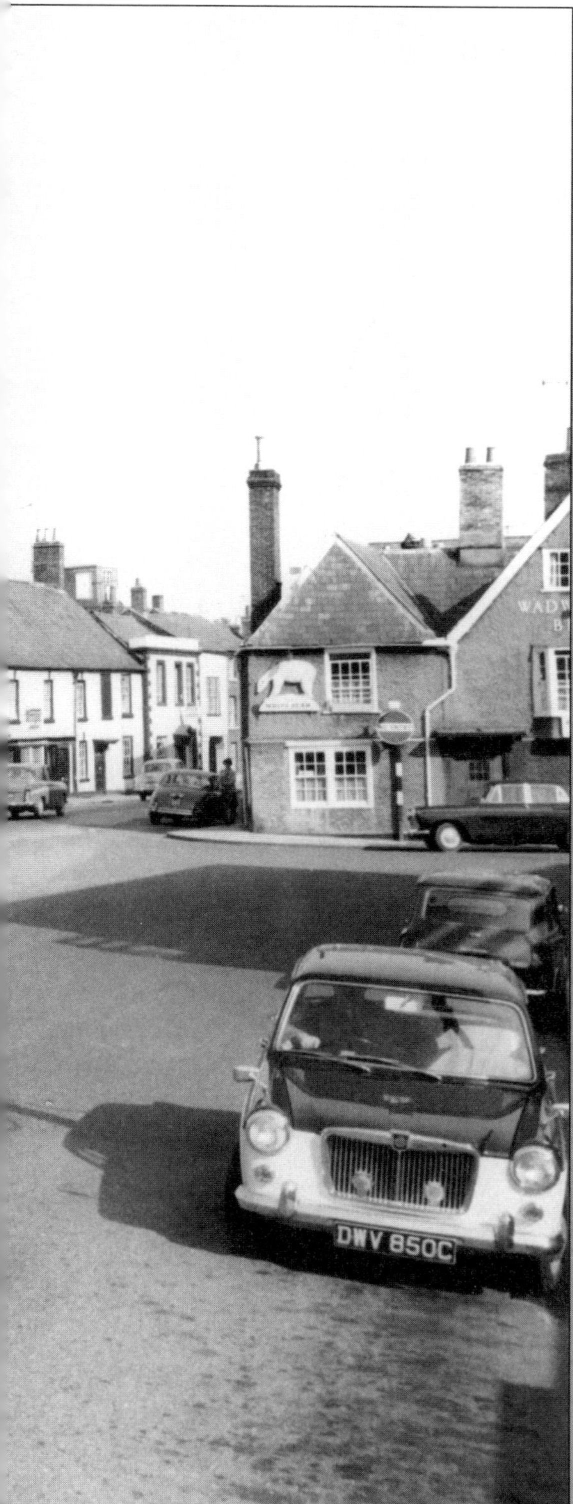

Monday Market Street leads off the junction at Maryport Street, Sheep Street and Sidmouth Street. It once formed part of the medieval market area, which included the space outside St Mary's Church. The market cross stood at the corner of the White Bear Inn (D28090, left), formerly known as the Talbot until 1673. One of the oldest houses in town is Great Porch House (D28090, centre), a beautiful half-timbered building built in the middle of the 15th century for a merchant. It has 17th century and later additions.

Until 1825, Sidmouth Street (D28088, pages 50-51) was known as Chapel Corner Street, and for a period was also called Leg o' Mutton Street. It was renamed after Henry Addington, Viscount Sidmouth, MP and Prime Minister. Sidmouth Street leads out of town towards the Green and St James' church. The increase in the volume of traffic continues to be a problem, along with the need for on-street parking and easy access to shops and businesses.

The London Road is a busy route with traffic coming from Calne, Marlborough and Swindon. Although road developments have addressed the increase in volume of traffic coming in and out of town, this area, known as Southbroom, has remained unspoilt, particularly the parts round the Green and St James' church. Again, the listed buildings status has preserved the area's beauty and history. The busy corner we see in D28086, pages 54-55, which is now part of Southbroom Road, shows the traffic before the roundabouts were laid out. Rose's the ironmongers is on the left, on the corner of Estcourt Street. The forecourt of the Blue Star Garage is on the right, now Kwik-Fit.

There is evidence of a Roman settlement in the Southbroom area of Devizes. As the town grew, it expanded into the area of the Green. There is an almost village feel to this part of town, with the church, the green and the swans on the Crammer, even though there used to be a foundry and a brewery here.

The North Wilts Foundry of Brown and May, once situated in an area off Estcourt Street, produced portable steam engines, traction engines for agricultural and road use, and pumps for water-works. The Estcourt Brewery stood where Morrisons now stands; it was the largest in the town until Wadworth took it over in 1903. You could say that for some people in the town, beer is in their blood. Rachel Multon, who works at Wadworth in Northgate Street, is the great-grand-daughter of Decimus Wild, who ran the brewery from 1861 to 1903. Her grandfather Harry Wiltshire was a talented artist who painted the signs for Wadworth's public houses.

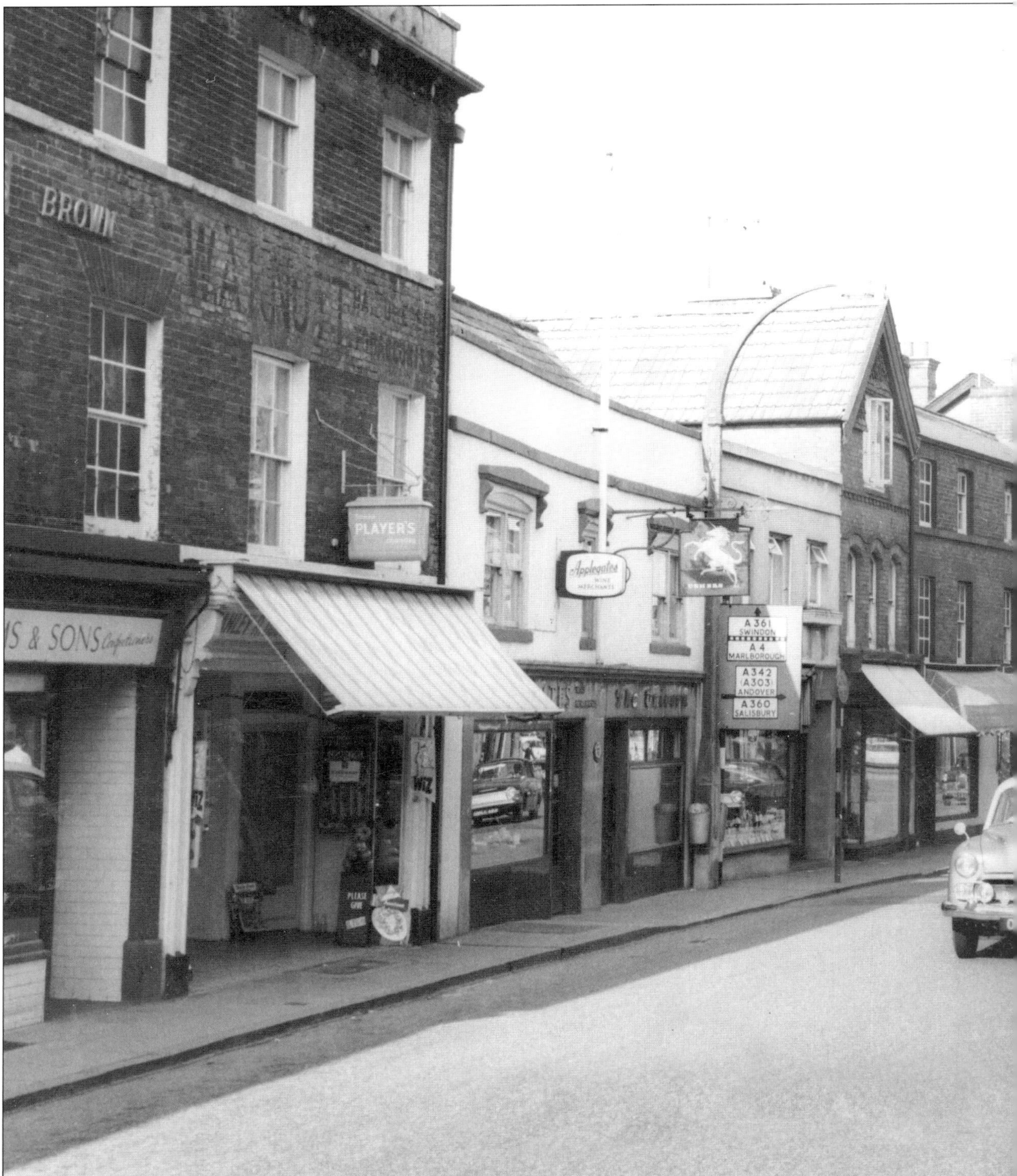
BROWN
PLAYER'S
Applegates
WINE MERCHANTS
A361
SWINDON
A4
MARLBOROUGH
A342
(A303)
ANDOVER
A360
SALISBURY

SIDMOUTH STREET c1960 D28088

The car dominates this street then and now. The premises on the left include a tobacconist, a public house, a grocer, a draper, a TV and radio shop, a ladies' clothes shop and a footwear shop. At the end of the street across the road is Rose's the ironmongers, a family-run business since 1947.

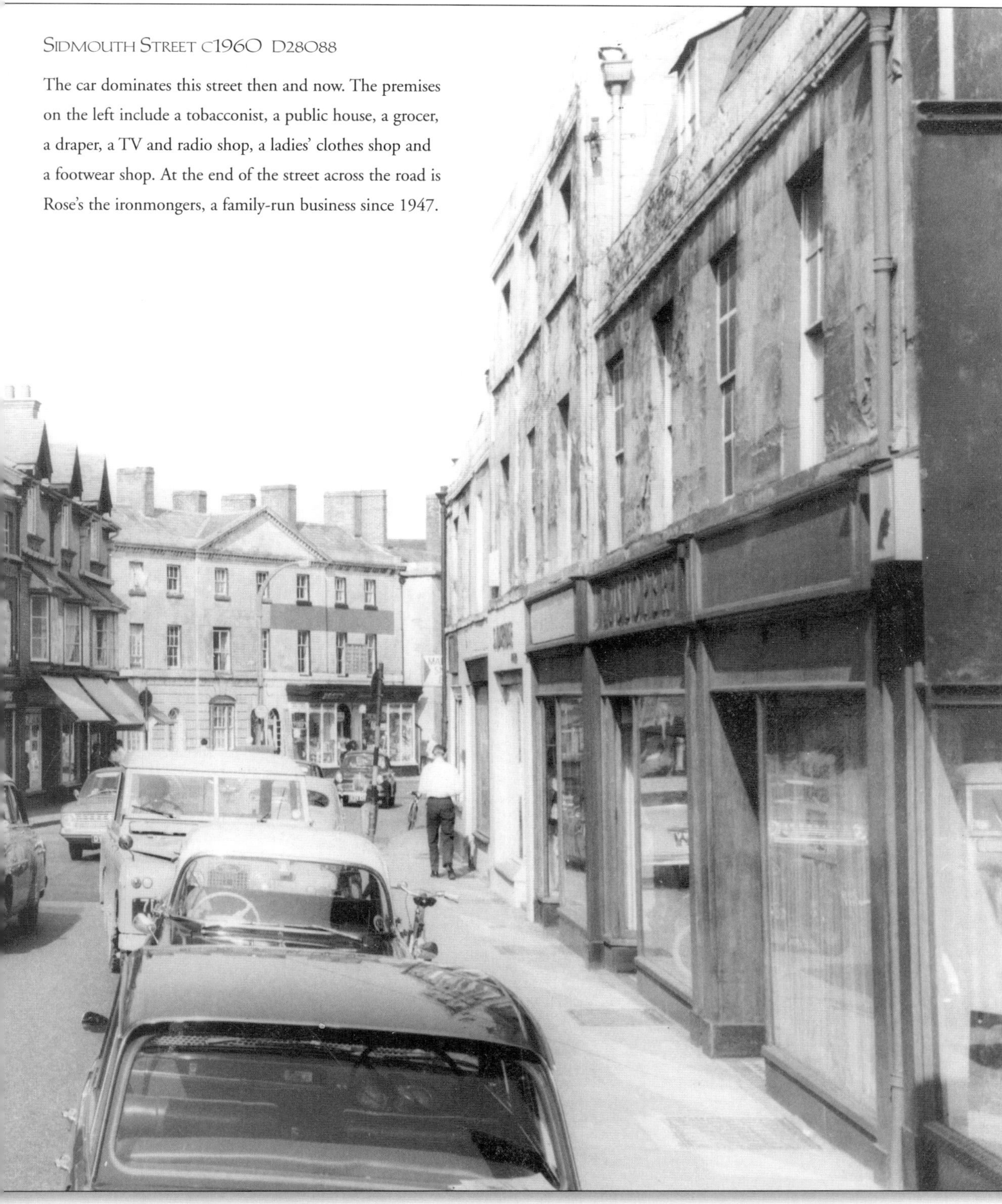

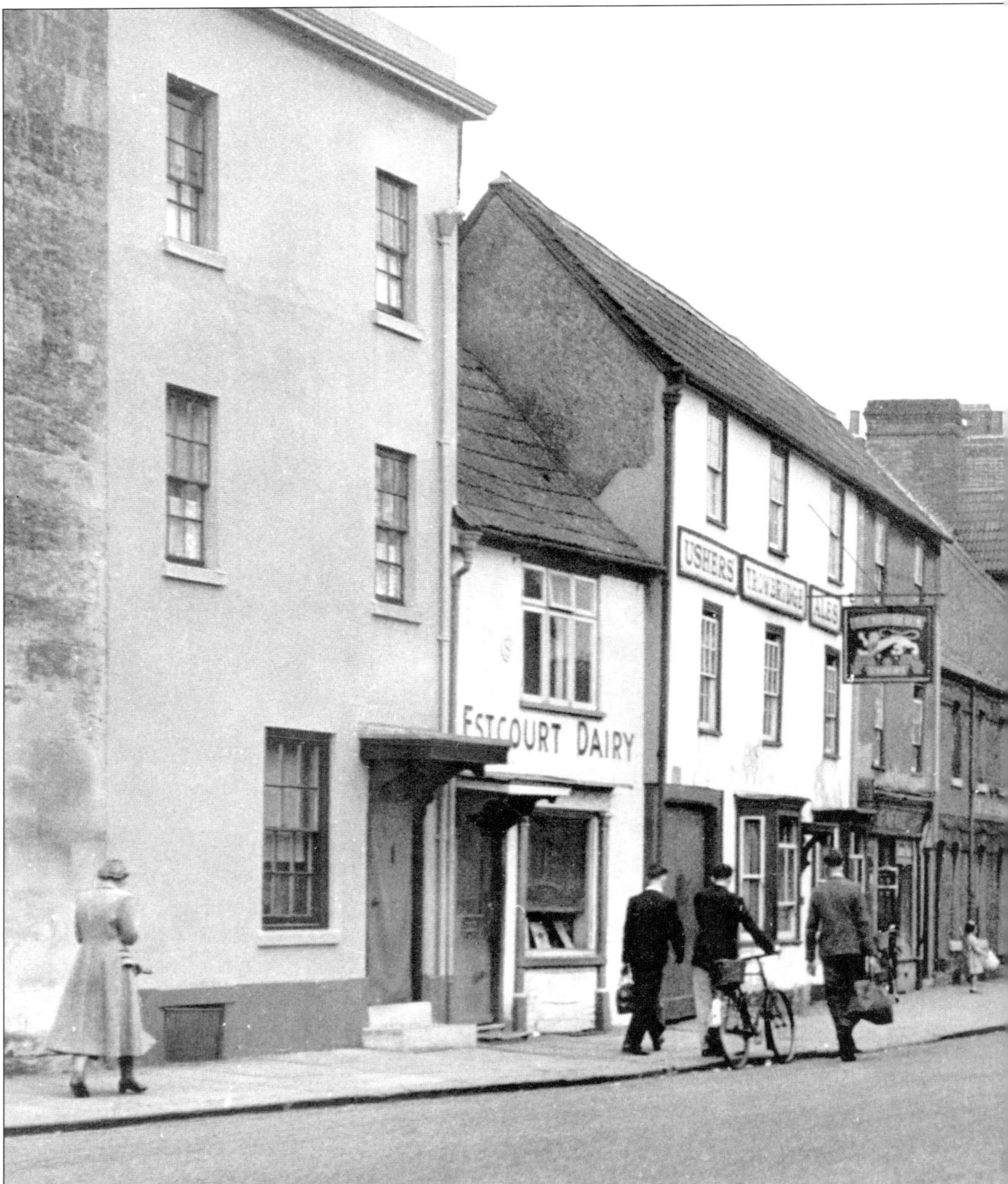
ESTCOURT DAIRY
USHERS
TROWBRIDGE
ALES

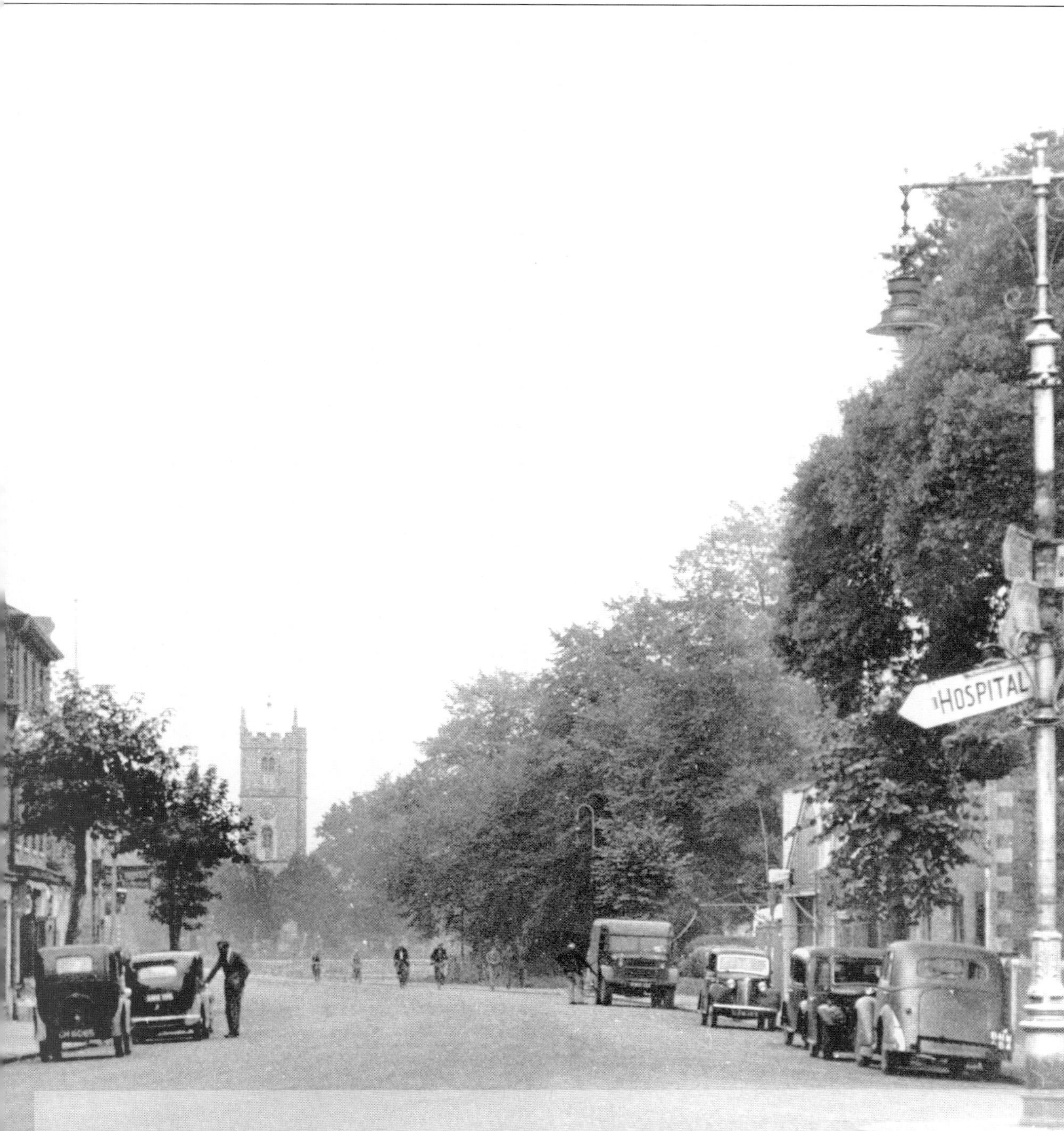

ESTCOURT STREET c1955 D28063

This view shows the road layout, sign posts and lighting before modernisation. In spite of the cars, it has a village feel to it, with pedestrians and cyclists unaffected by traffic. The British Lion public house next to the Estcourt Dairy is early 18th-century.

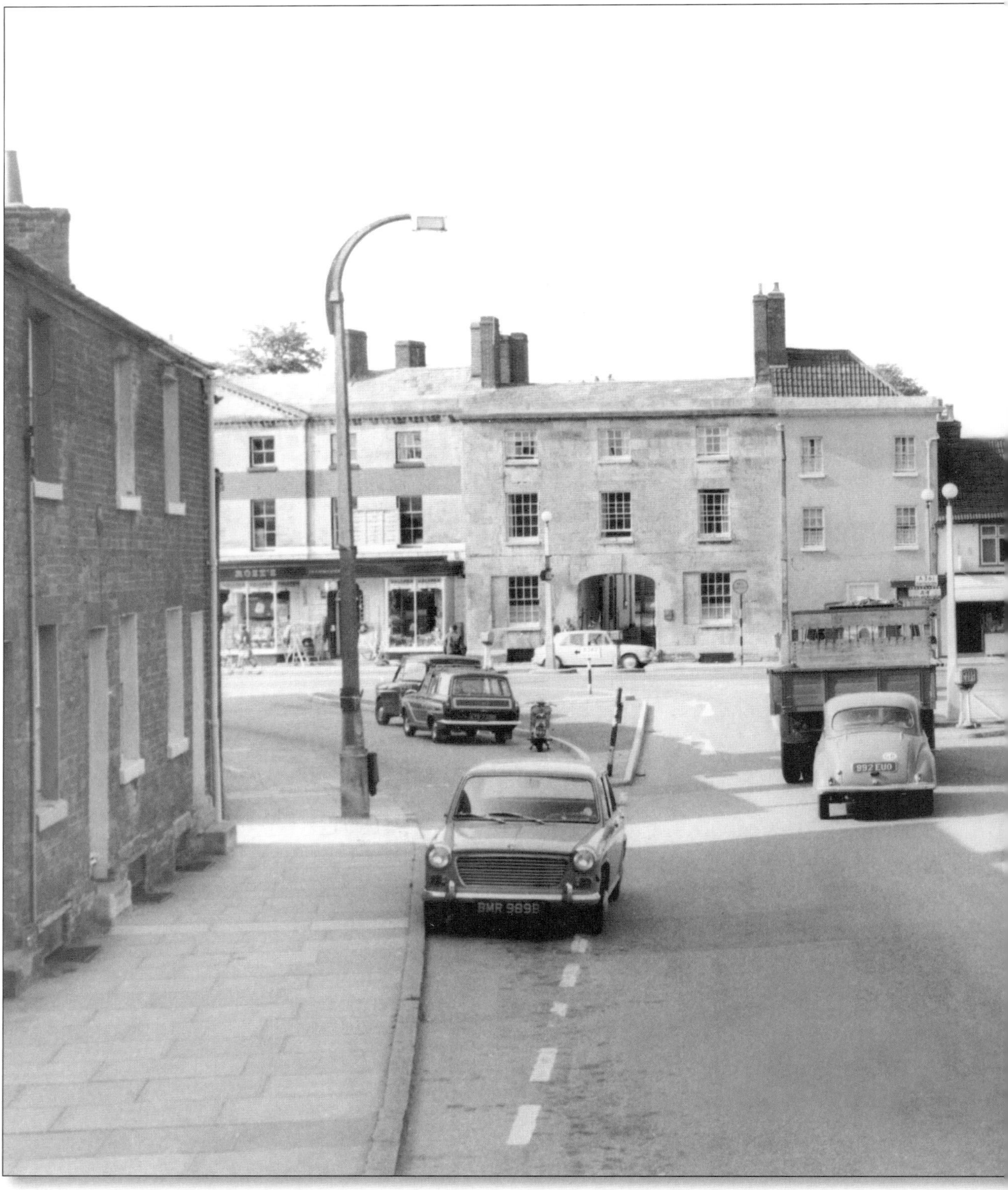

Southbroom Place c1960 D28086

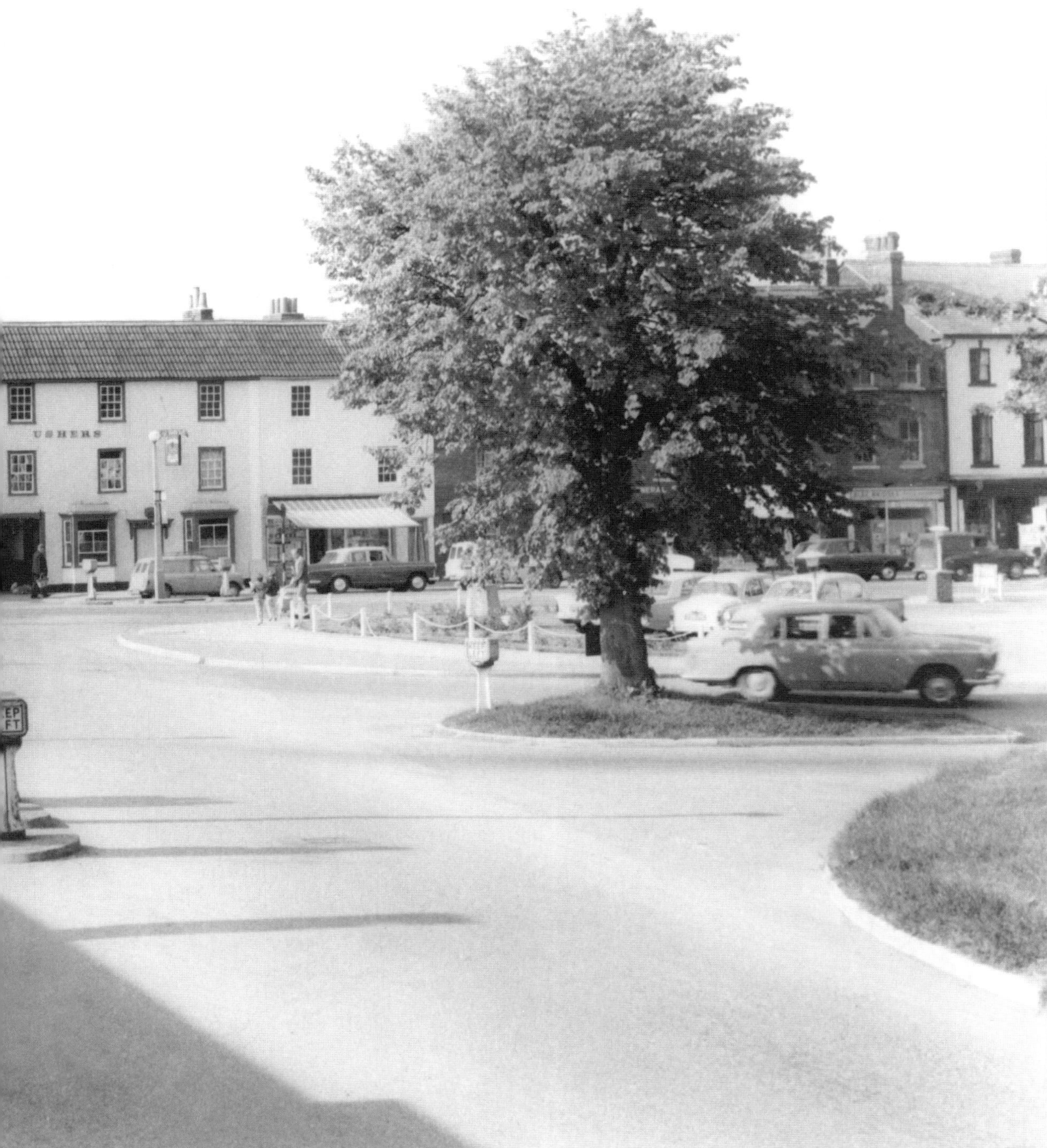

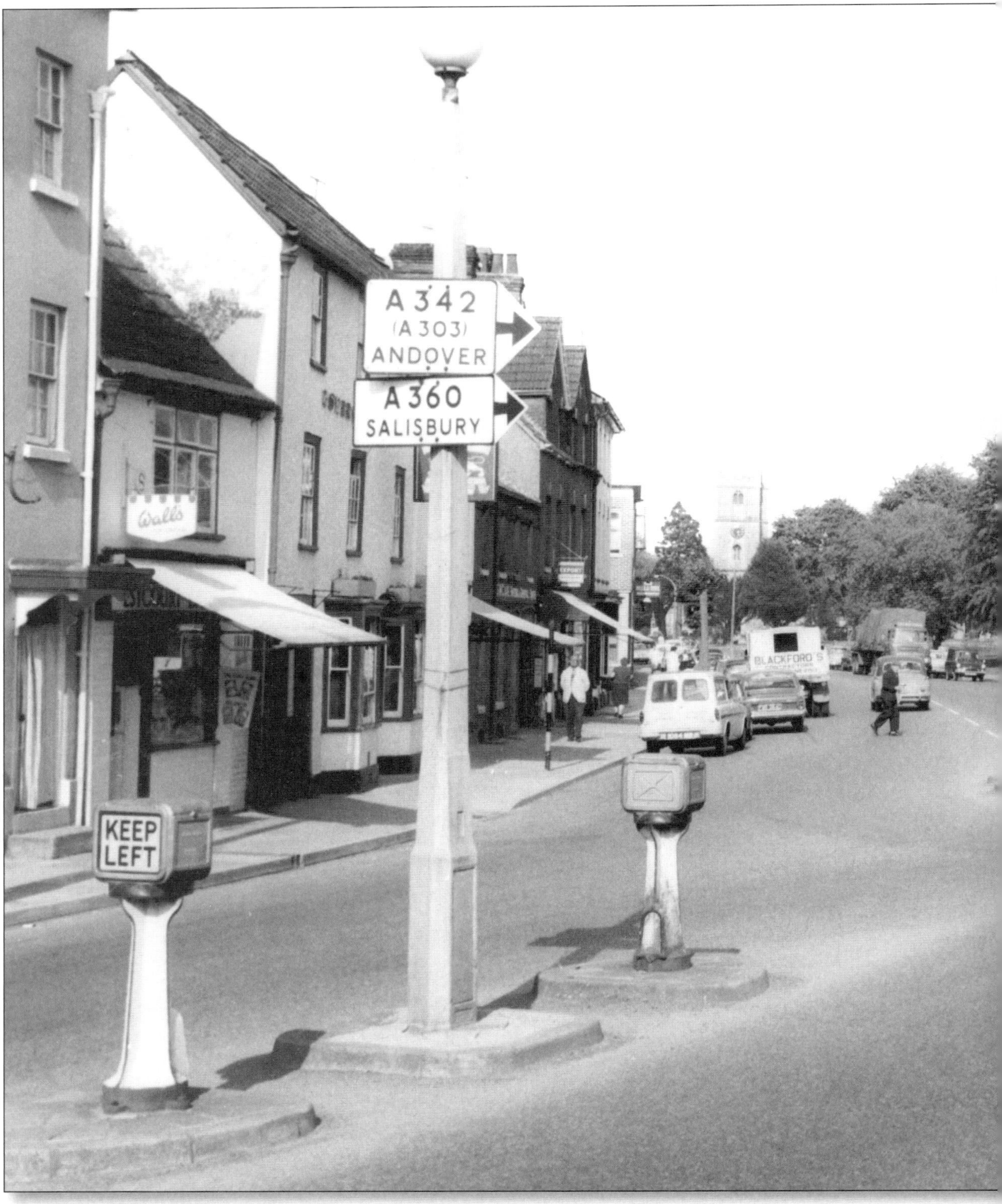
A342
(A303)
ANDOVER
A360
SALISBURY
KEEP LEFT
Wall's
BLACKFORD'S

THE BRITTOX TO ESTCOURT STREET

ESTCOURT STREET c1960 D28087

The traffic islands were known locally as 'the silly islands' when they were first built. The unsupported front of the Blue Star Garage was quite a feature when it was first erected. The statue of Queen Victoria, which still stands on the corner, was taken from the front of the stone mason's house, Victoria Cottage, with the scaffolding (beyond the garage).

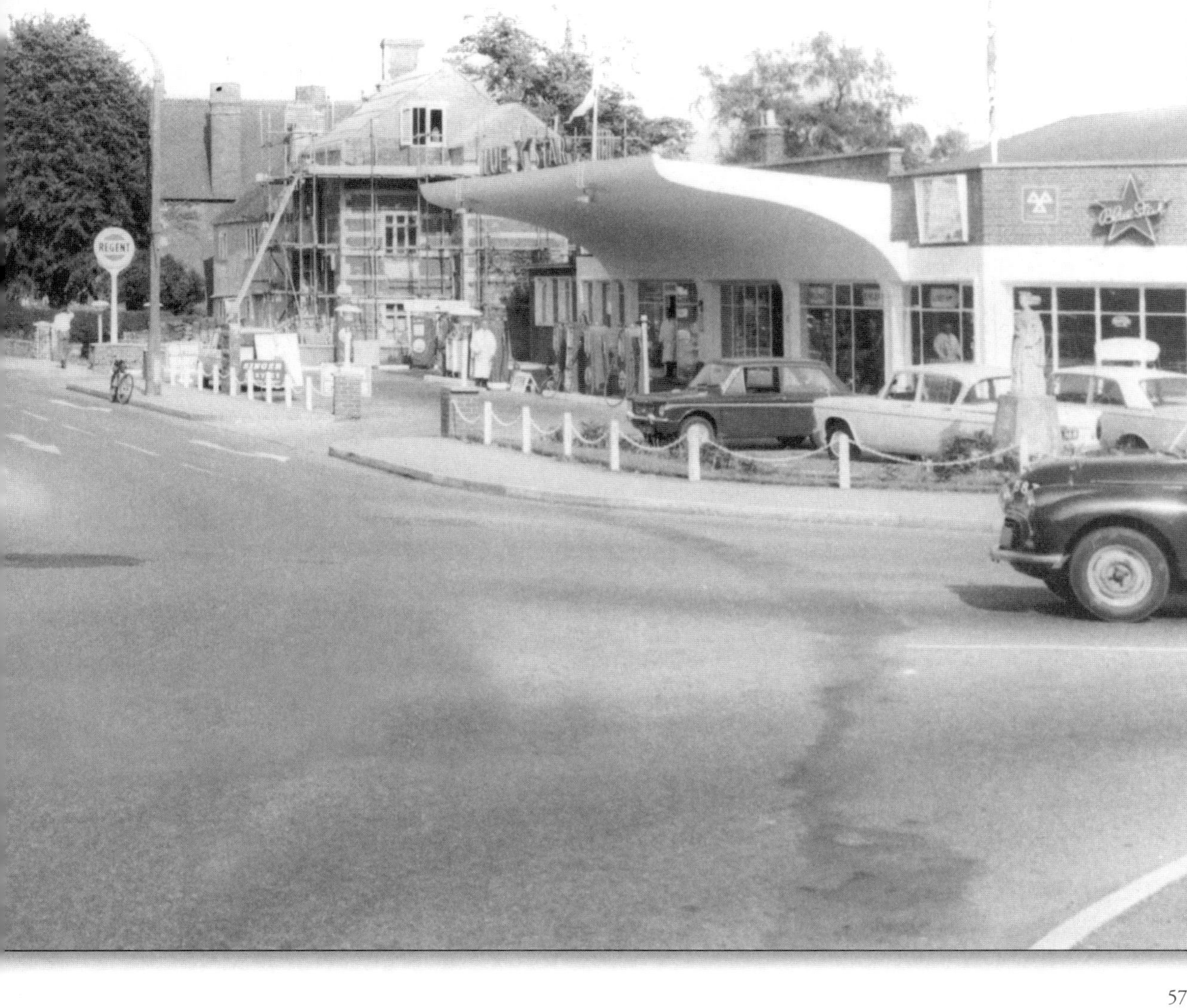

THE BELLS RING OUT - THE CHURCHES

One of the best-loved parts of Devizes is the area around the Green and the Crammer. The view across to the church of St James, Southbroom, nestling among the trees, is one of the prettiest in Wiltshire.

The origin of the name 'Crammer' is not clear. Some say it comes from the Anglo Saxon word 'krames', which related to an arcade of booths at a fair where the articles on sale were called 'kramerie'. Others believe it came from a Dame Cramer who lived nearby, or from Cranes' Pond, because it was a favourite spot for those birds.

The Green has changed little. It is a popular place for walking, playing and just sitting and enjoying the view. It is common ground, but for a period it was owned by T Sotheron Estcourt after an Act of Parliament allowed common land to be bought by individuals. For centuries it has been a venue for fairs and markets.

St James' Church is the third Protestant church in town. It was first mentioned in 1461, and was dedicated in 1505. It possibly occupied the site of a former leper hospital. It was largely rebuilt in 1831 to designs by the architect John Peniston from Salisbury, at a cost of £1,053. The tower is the only original part left of the 15th-century church which Arthur Mee described in his volume on Wiltshire in his 'The King's England' series in 1965: 'it is the best tower in the town and is one of a group of five in Wiltshire which have the top stage panelled and the centre of the panelling pierced to let out the sound of the bells'.

It became the garrison church in 1878 when the Le Marchant Barracks were built and became the home of the Wiltshire Regiment. The colours and memorials of the Wiltshire Regiment, some from the Boer War, are displayed in the army corner. The organ and organ loft have been beautifully restored. The interior of the church is bright and airy, and the ceiling and the embossed ribbing have been beautifully painted in blue and gold.

ST JAMES' CHURCH 1898 42316

A perfect Wiltshire scene. This shows the Crammer at low water level.

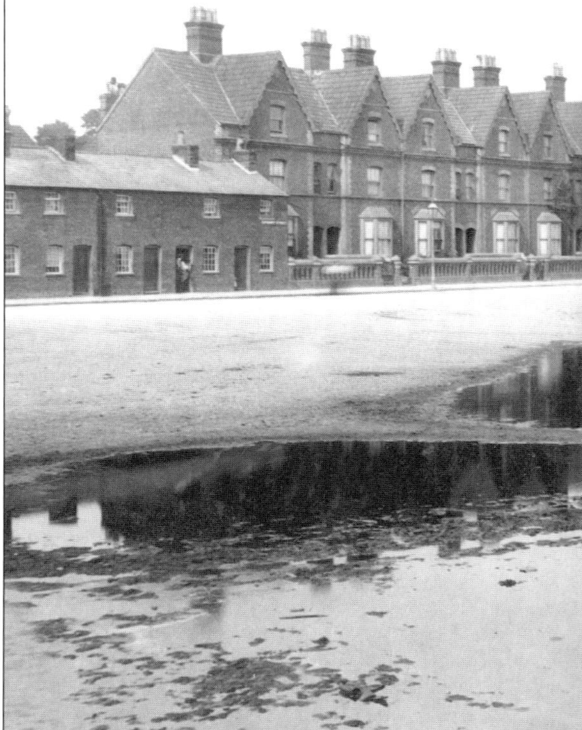

THE CRAMMER AND ST JAMES' CHURCH c1960 D28076

Swans are a familiar sight on the Crammer pond. In 1967 the Crammer was walled in, but the wall was soon removed as a result of public protest.

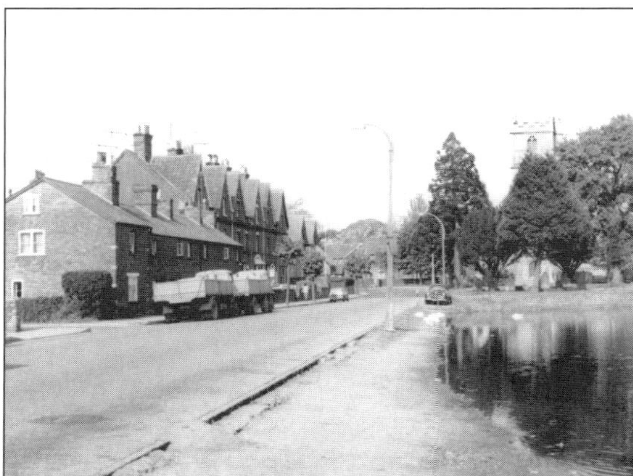

THE BELLS RING OUT - THE CHURCHES

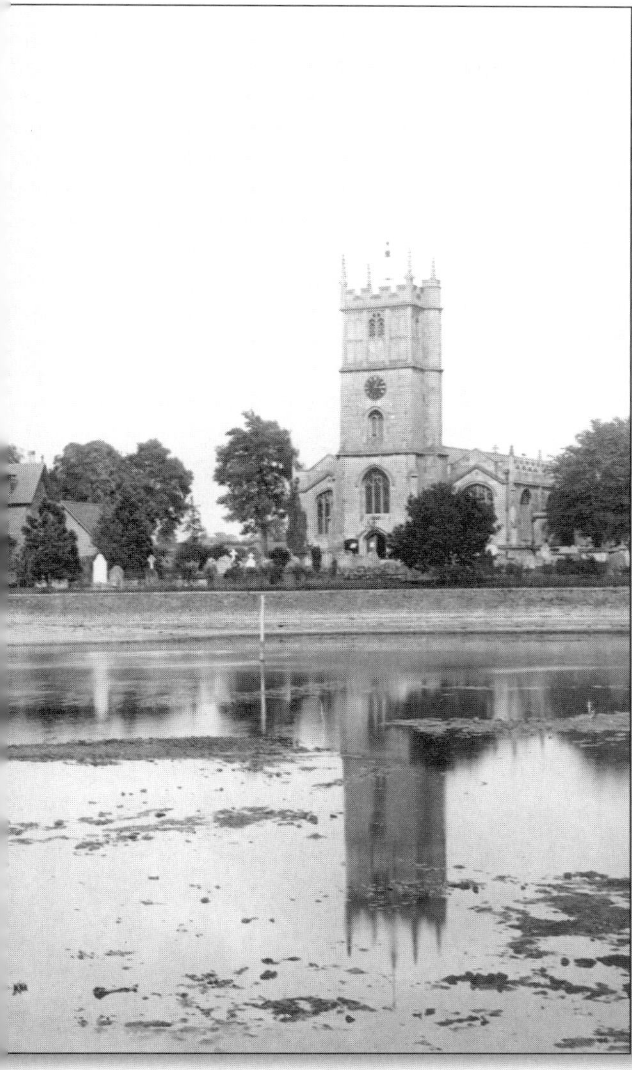

Devizes has more of its share of fine churches than most Wiltshire towns of similar size. Lorna Haycock forwards the evidence that St John the Baptist's church was built later than St Mary the Virgin's church. The former was built to accommodate the castle population and garrison; the latter was built possibly on the site of a former small church for the expanding town. Other restoration work took place in the 1840s and 1850s. The present churches still retain their original plan and many of their original features.

Pevsner wrote of St John's Church: 'a major Norman church, dominated by a mighty crossing tower with round stair-turret higher than the tower. Big Norman windows with decorated arches.' The magnificent approach from St John's Court can be seen on page 43, the view shows the medieval hall on the right, one of the oldest buildings in Devizes. It was the home of Mayor Thomas Coventry, who died in 1451. It was partially rebuilt in the 17th century, and was refronted in 1842 using stone from St John's church.

The original church was a Norman cruciform structure consisting of chancel, nave, transepts and central tower. In the middle of the 15th century the nave was rebuilt and aisles added. Later, the north and south chapels to the chancel were also added. Today the church consists of a chancel of two bays, with the Lamb Chapel in the north bay and the Beauchamp Chapel in the south bay; the central tower, with north and south transept; and a nave of six bays.

There is a wonderful richness of colour and texture in the church. It is worth looking closely at the nail-studded doors as we enter, which date from 15th century. The interlaced arches with the zigzag pattern in the sanctuary (42305, centre, page 64) date from Norman times. The high altar and steps are made of Purbeck marble. The organ in the north transept is housed in a beautifully-carved case, possibly the work of Grinling Gibbons. There are interesting and amusing carvings: the Green Man, a relic of pagan tree worship, peeps out from the top of a pillar in the choir; grotesque faces look down from walls in the Beauchamp Chapel.

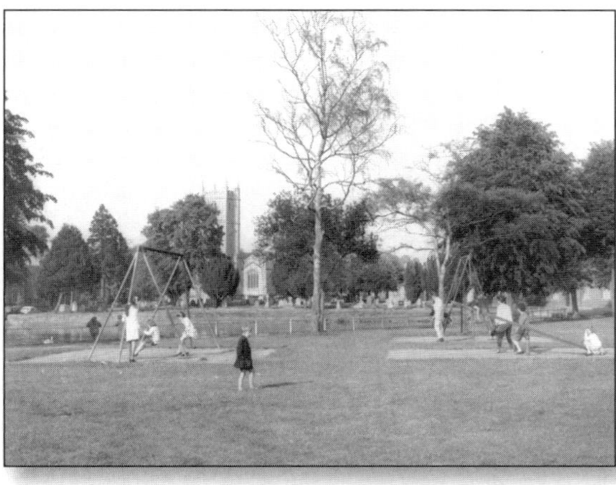

THE GREEN C1965 D28097

This part, known as 'the Little Green', is a children's play area. It has been modernised recently; the equipment was changed to meet current Health and Safety regulations.

THE BELLS RING OUT - THE CHURCHES

Little has altered over the years in and around the church. There are some fine old gravestones and monuments in the churchyard, although many of them are hard to read now, sad to say. A new monument, the Devizes Millennium Cross by the sculptor Eric Stanford, has recently been erected, and will undoubtedly become an important part of the town's history.

Across town stands the other fine church, St Mary's (pages 66-67), which is approached from New Park Street. It was originally built next to the town's first market place in the 12th century, and was largely rebuilt in the 15th century. It is recognisably Norman, as Pevsner notes, by the flat buttresses, the corbel-table and the square stone blocks. Like St John's, it has a Norman chancel. Above the porch door is an unusual carving of a woman struggling with a monster. The tower is 91ft high and 14ft square, and contains a peal of six bells dating from 1663. High up on the east end of the nave roof is a medieval statue of the Virgin and Child.

Inside, the visitor is aware of the generous proportions, with the lofty arcades and the Norman features. There is an unusual star-shaped vaulted tower ceiling which has a central hole giving access to the bells. The fine nave roof bears a gold-painted Latin inscription around its edge, asking us to pray for the soul of William Smyth who rebuilt the church and who died in 1436. Restoration work has revealed traces of biblical paintings on the chancel walls.

Whilst Nonconformism developed in Devizes, and some of the chapels remain, the movement did not take hold as much as it did elsewhere in the county. Charles Wesley preached in the town in the 1740s, and was received with a considerable amount of hostility. There was a Quaker settlement in the late 17th century.

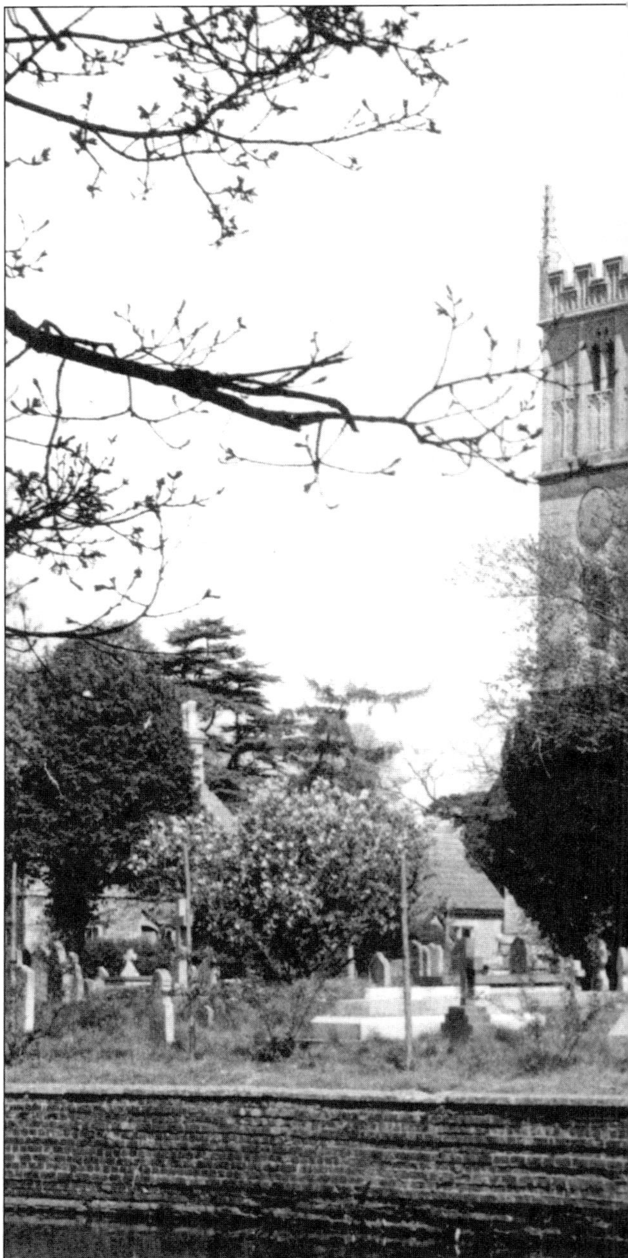

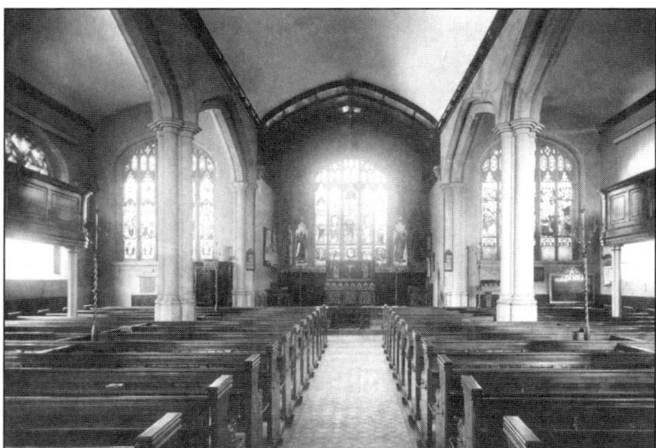

LEFT: ST JAMES' CHURCH, THE INTERIOR 1898 42317

The galleries that run along the sides have since been removed. The colours and memorials of the Wiltshire Regiment are displayed in the army corner, right in picture.

THE BELLS RING OUT - THE CHURCHES

ST JAMES' CHURCH AND THE POND, FROM CHURCH WALK C1955

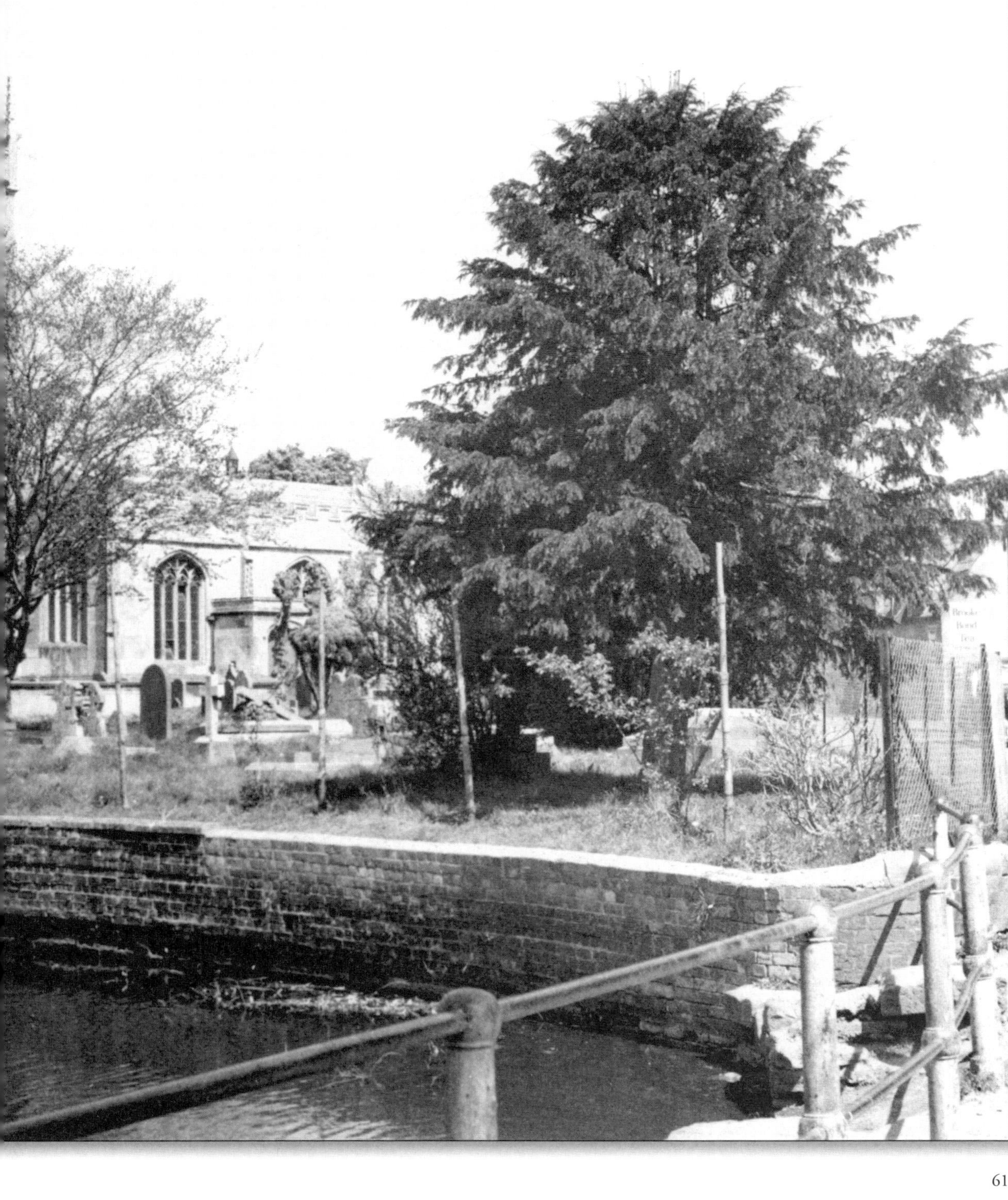

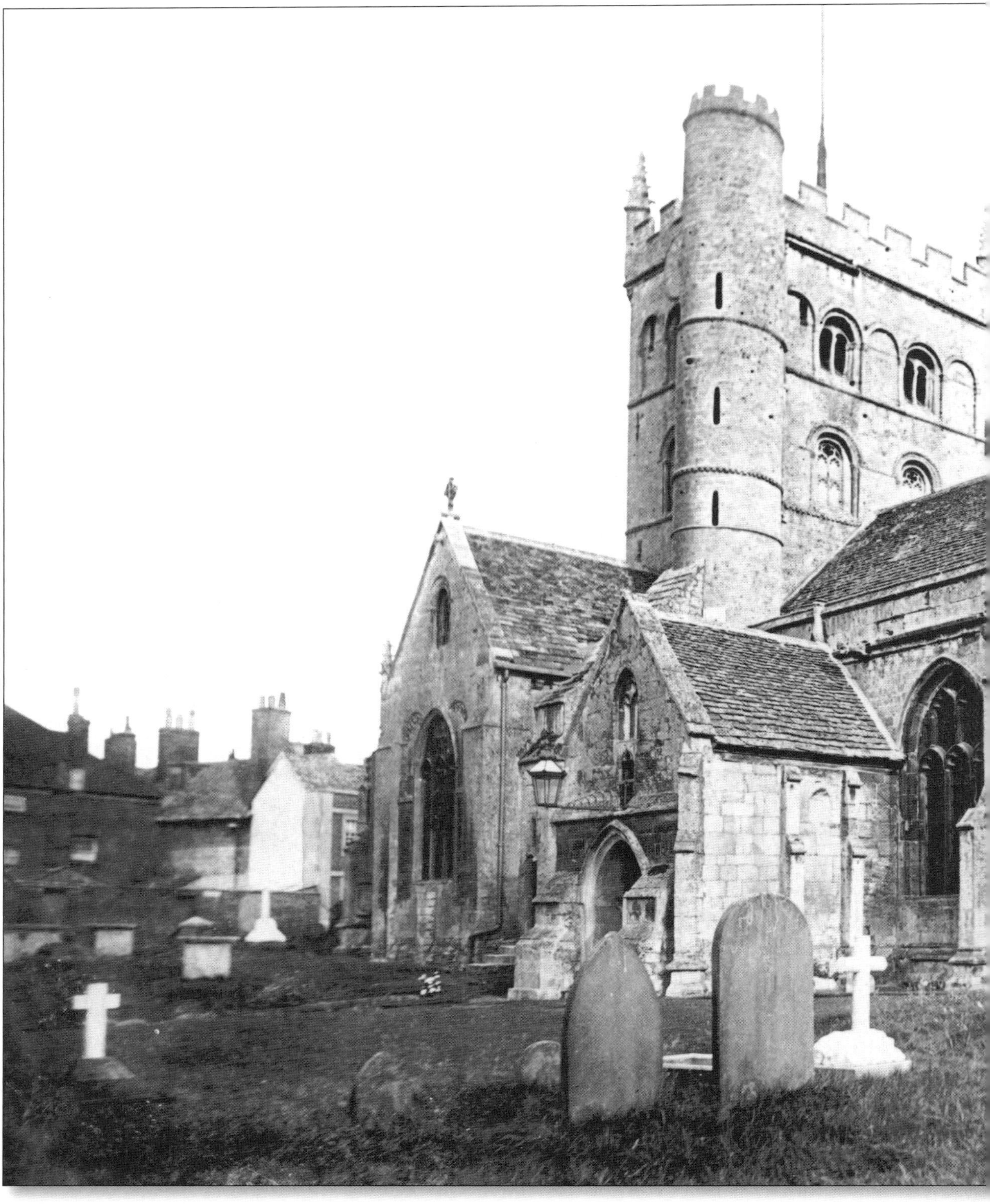

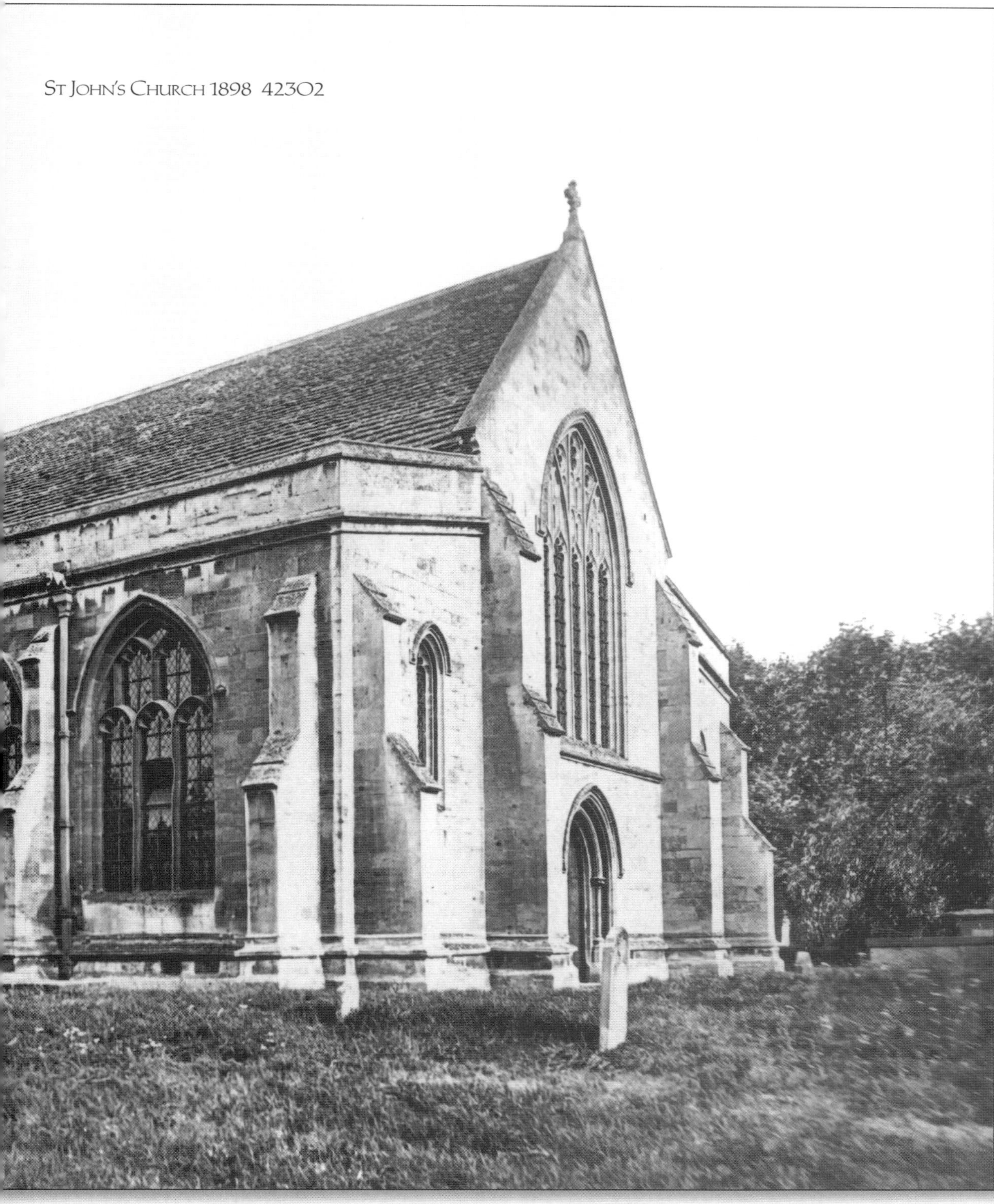

ST JOHN'S CHURCH 1898 42302

THE BELLS RING OUT - THE CHURCHES

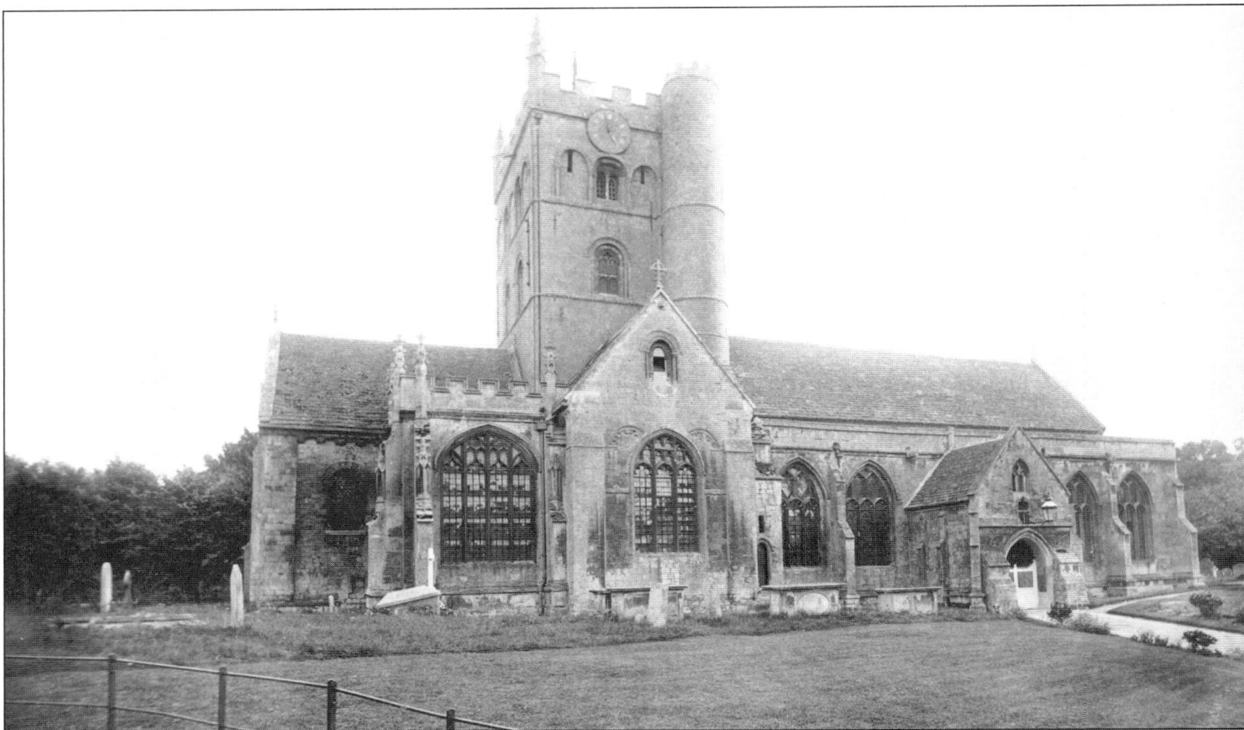

Above: ST JOHN'S CHURCH 1898 42303

The fine features mentioned by Pevsner can be appreciated in this photograph and 42304 opposite. The present day view is partially obscured by trees and the railings and lantern have been removed.

ST JOHN'S, THE INTERIOR 1898 42305

The pulpit incorporates some 14th-century panels, and now stands on a modern wooden base. Pevsner rather sadly describes the nave arcades as 'disappointingly scraped'. The ordinary visitor may, however, decide that they are fine and graceful and worth a closer look. The colours of the Devizes Loyal Volunteers hang above the chancel.

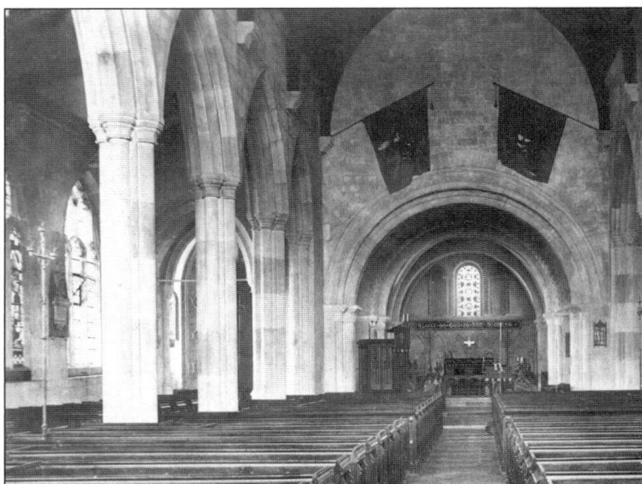

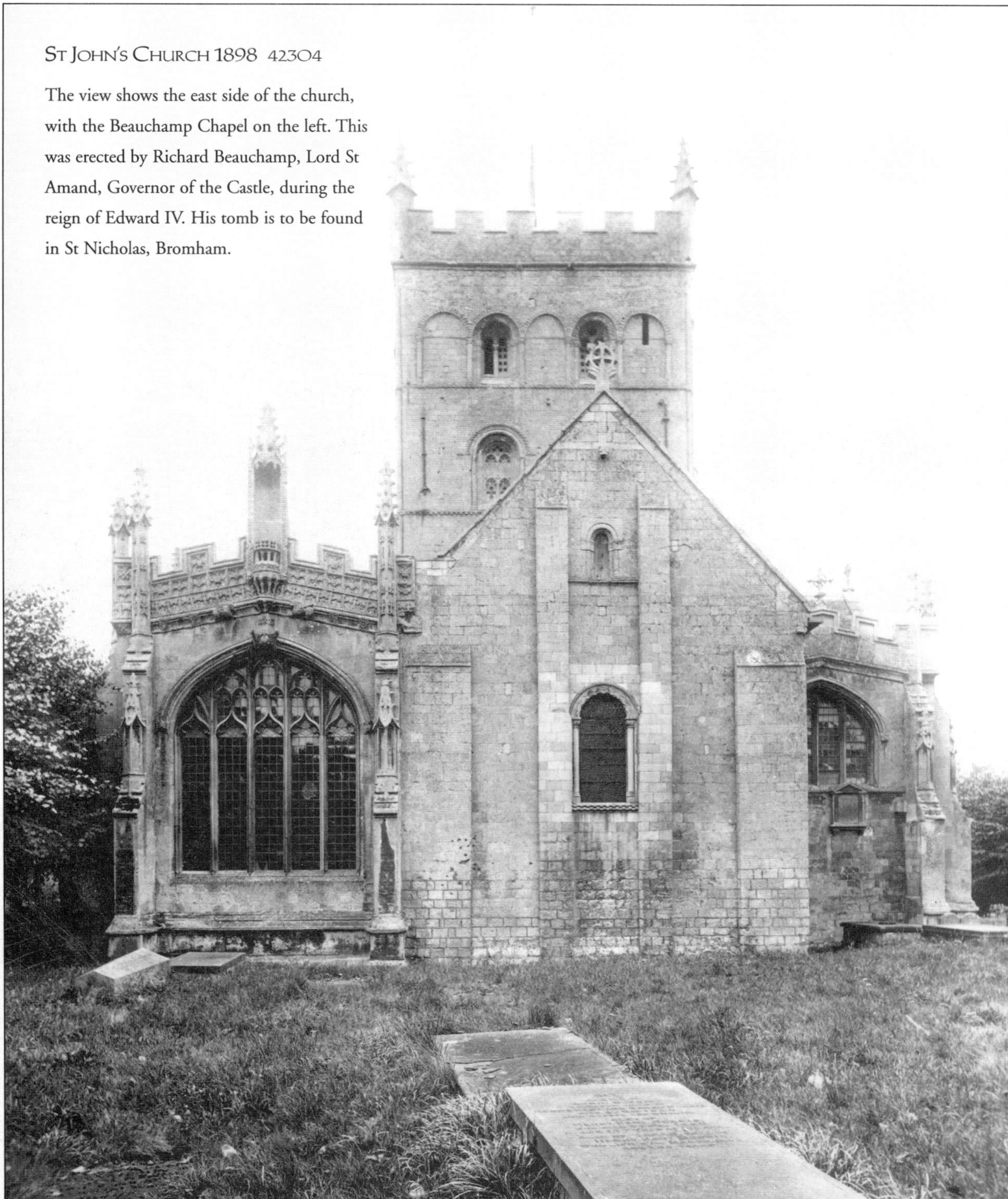

ST JOHN'S CHURCH 1898 42304

The view shows the east side of the church, with the Beauchamp Chapel on the left. This was erected by Richard Beauchamp, Lord St Amand, Governor of the Castle, during the reign of Edward IV. His tomb is to be found in St Nicholas, Bromham.

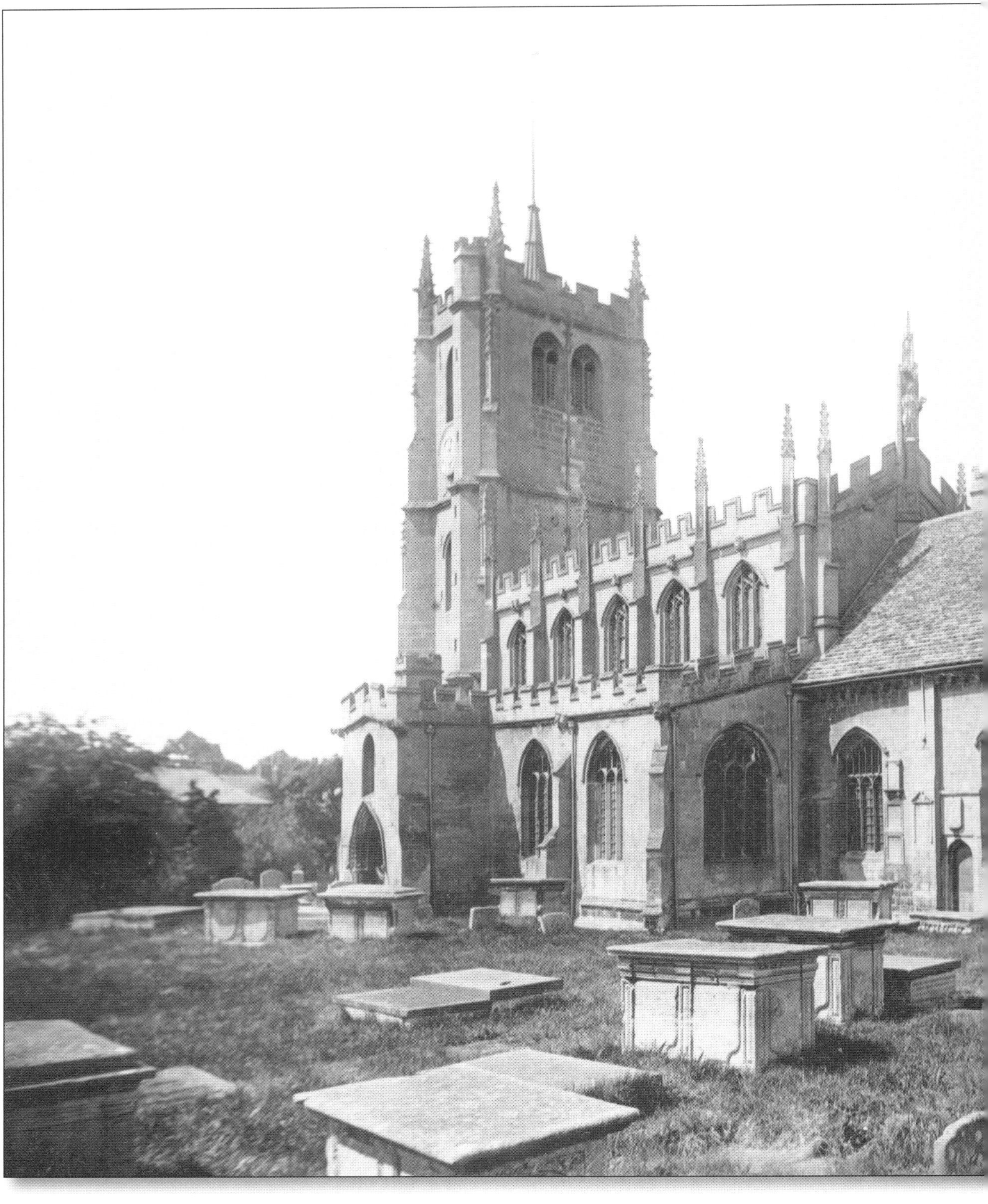

THE BELLS RING OUT - THE CHURCH

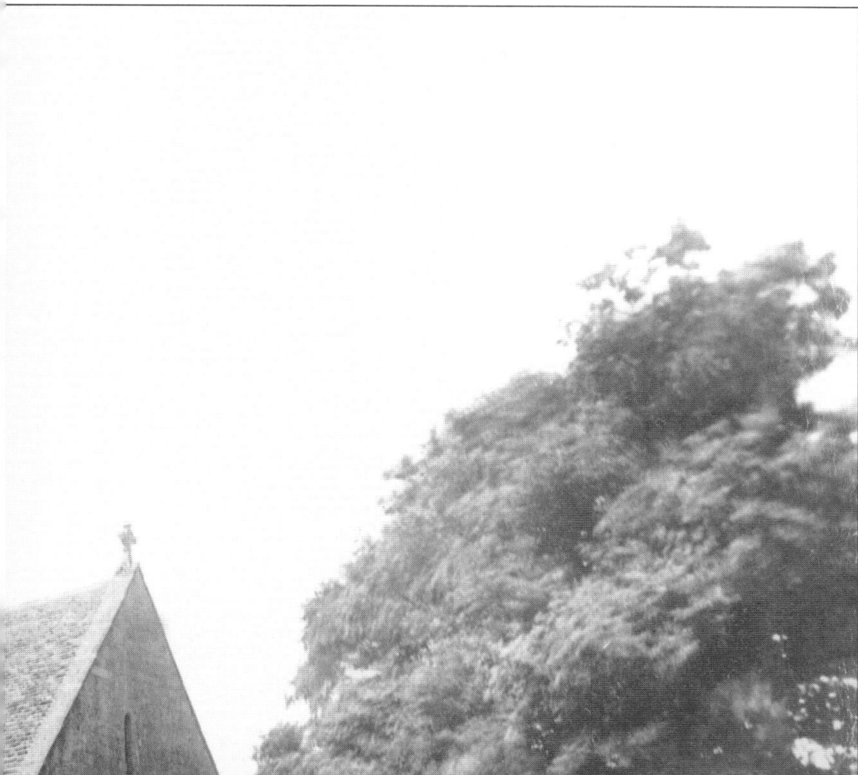

St Mary's Church 1898
42312

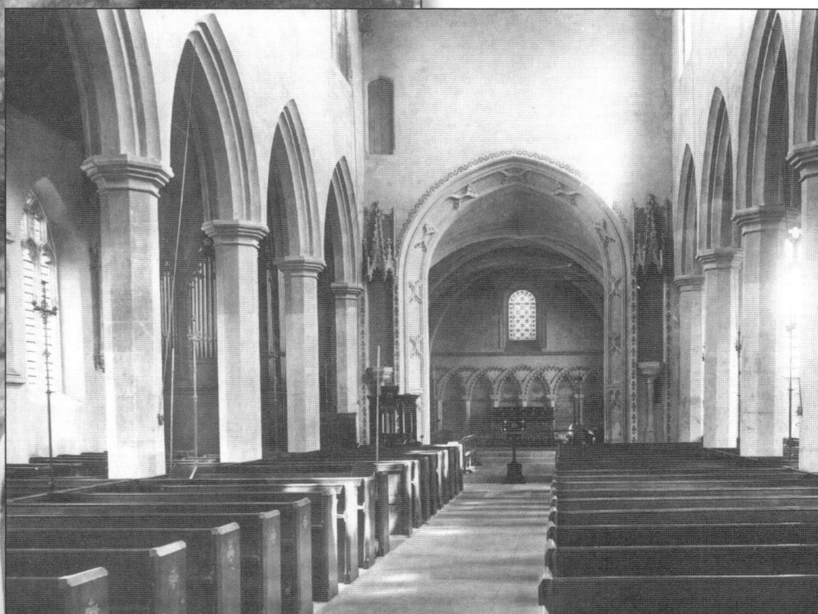

St Mary's Church Interior
1898 42313

The arch leading to the chancel has beautifully carved decoration. The coat of arms that is displayed on the chancel arch today bears the arms of George III and was restored in 1963. In the Middle Ages, the small door to the left of the arch led to the rood loft, where stood statues of the Virgin Mary and St John.

THE BELLS RING OUT - THE CHURCHES

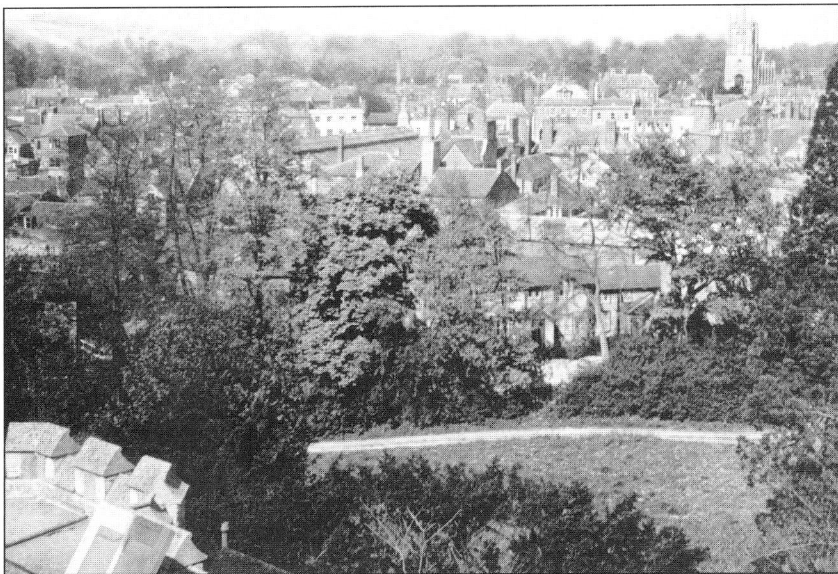

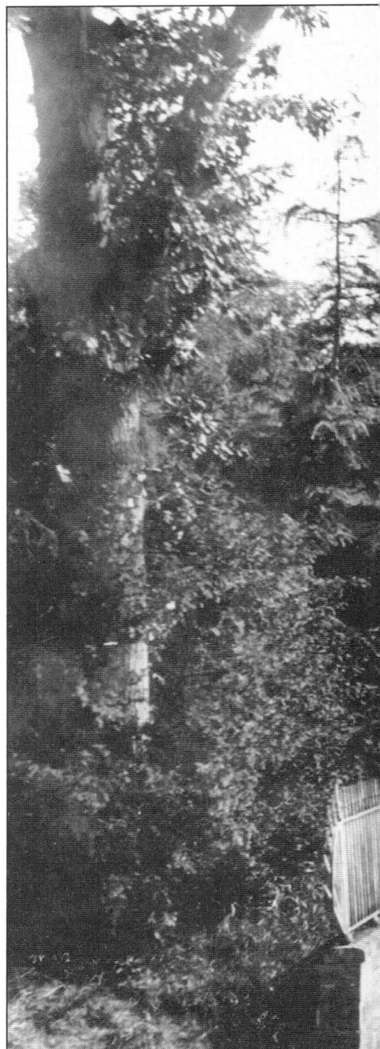

Above: THE VIEW FROM THE CASTLE c1955 D28048

St Mary's can be seen to the right. Slightly to the left is Brownston House, one of only two Grade I listed buildings in town. It was originally built in 1700, but was rebuilt later in 1720. It has seven bays with a three-bay projection and a hipped roof, and is well worth a visit. Pevsner called it 'the best house in Devizes'.

Right: ST MARY'S CHURCH 1898 42314

This photograph was taken from outside Quakers Walk Lodge. It shows an uninterrupted view to the church. The houses along New Park Road and Commercial Road were not built until the late 1920s. Stone urns were added to the gate posts at a later date.

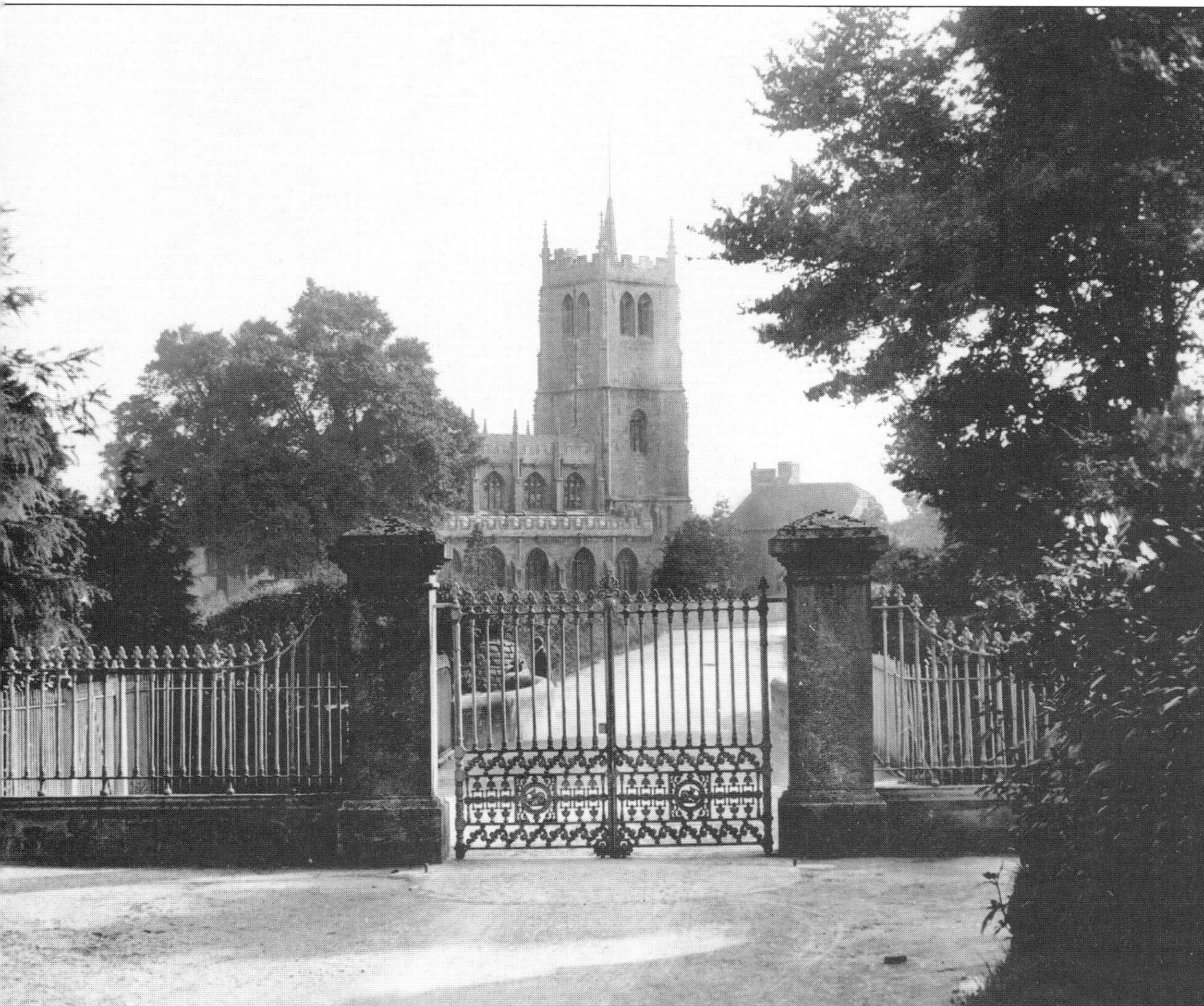

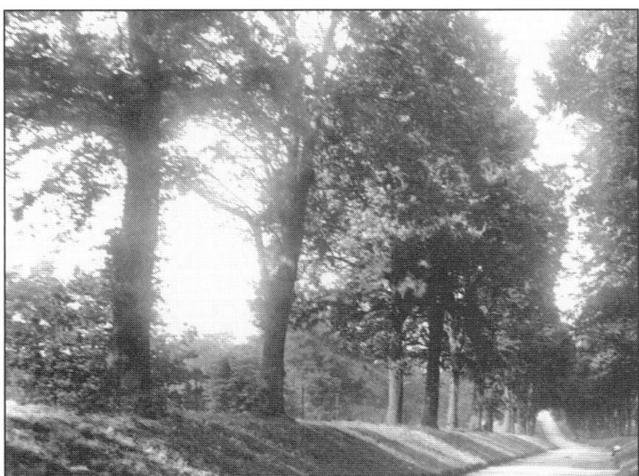

QUAKERS WALK 1898 42315

The name is probably a corruption of 'Keepers' Walk'. The long avenue of elms ran to Roundway Estate. Unfortunately, this area is now threatened by developers.

POWERFUL POSITIONS - CASTLE AND CANAL

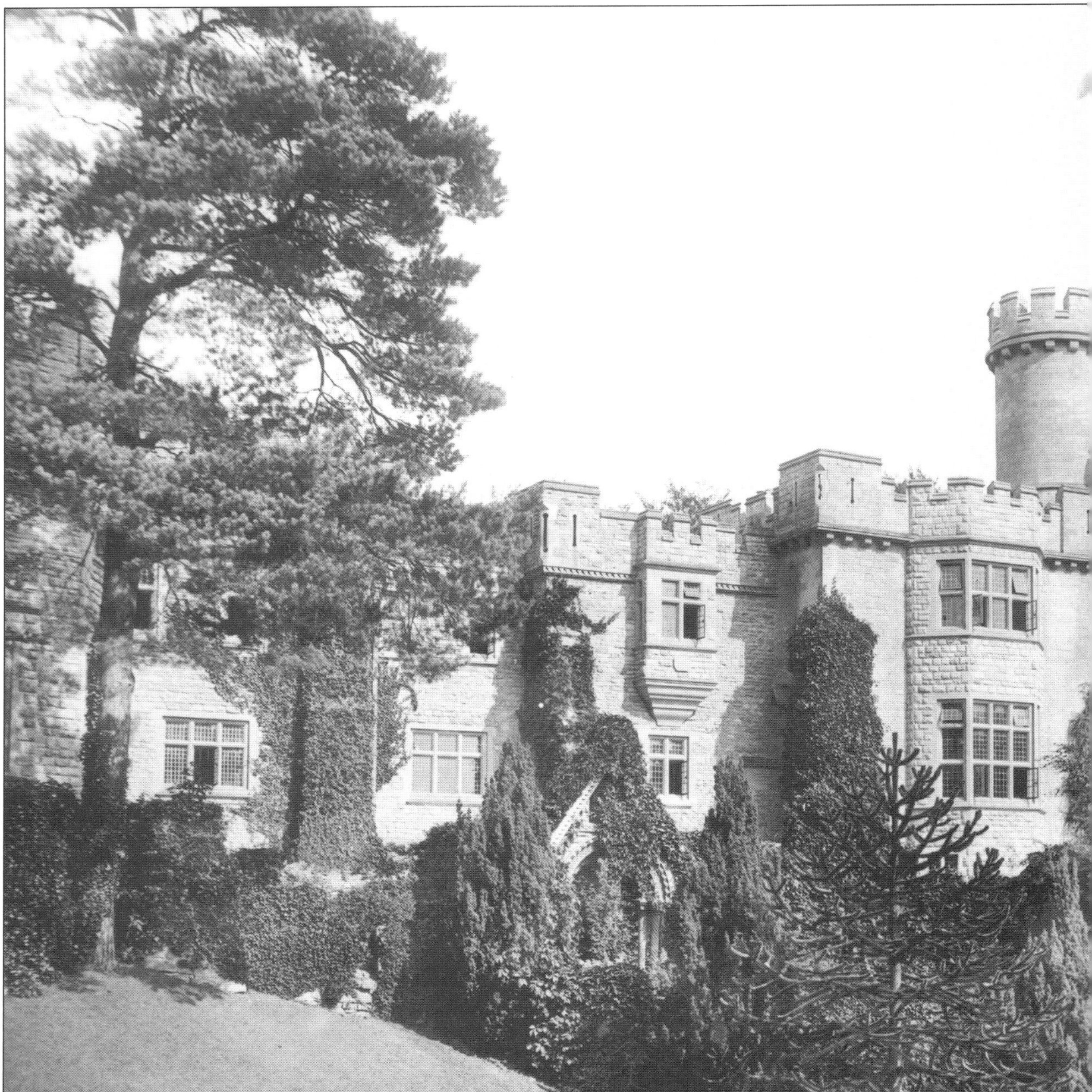

THE CASTLE 1898 42308

This view was taken looking towards the south side of the Watch Tower and Round Tower and the Mansion House. This was designed by A S Goodridge of Bath. A large circular keep was built on the site of the south tower, and battlements were added to the north tower.

POWERFUL POSITIONS - CASTLE AND CANAL

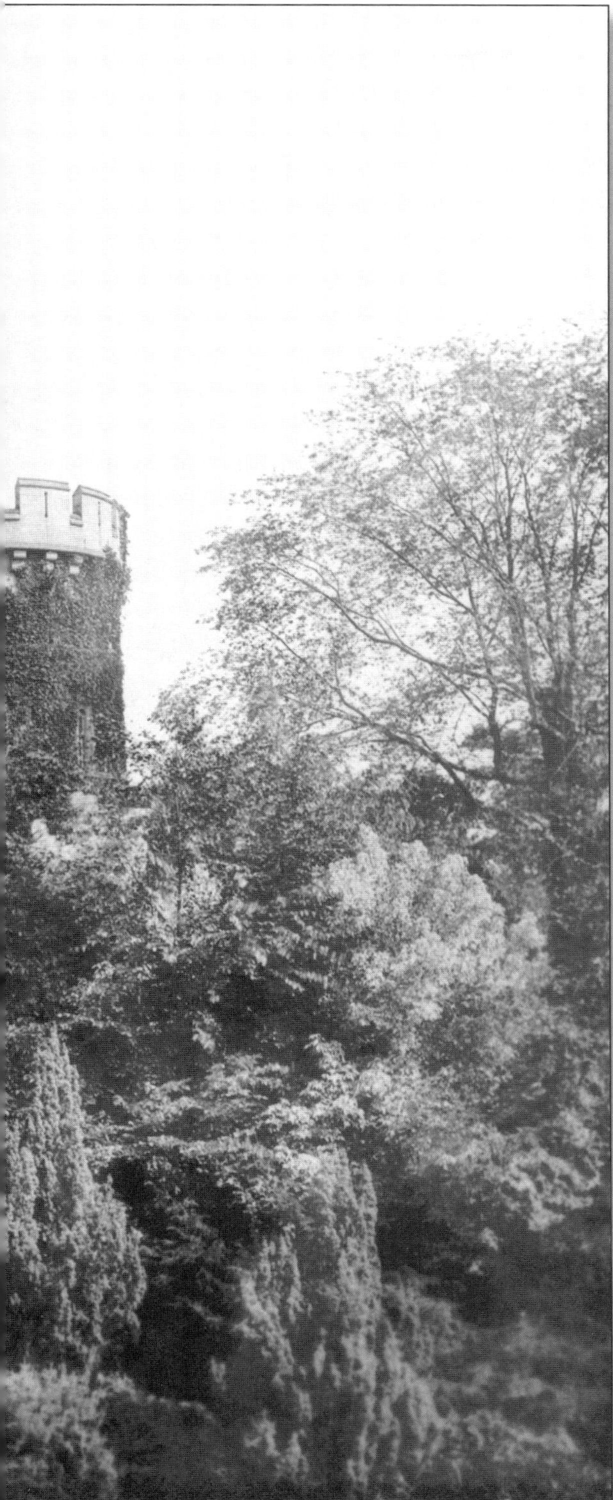

Devizes Castle is privately owned and not now open to the public. It is an impressive property which holds an important position in the town's history. Nearly two hundred years passed between the destruction of the Castle in the time of Cromwell and the start of the new building. In 1838, Valentine Leach, a local tradesman and prominent Nonconformist, bought the Castle estate from Thomas Tylee. He, and later his son Robert, transformed the place. Leach built the Round Tower which forms the southern part of the present mansion and preserved the northern windmill tower.

The site had been laid waste and was little more than a quarry. Many of the stones were removed for use on buildings in the town. A letter from 'Rusty Antiquarian', which appeared in the 'Devizes and Wiltshire Gazette' in August 1863, complained that 'there was perhaps never an ancient monument so completely dismantled or removed as our poor Castle! Not a stone available for building, fencing, or any other purpose to which stone material could be applied by builders, masons, or others was left unremoved!'

The 1883 sales brochure for Devizes Castle gives us an insight into this tantalising place. '10 bedrooms, connected with 2 are a boudoir and oratory. Bedroom accommodation for 6 servants'. Among its features were a study, a circular morning room, a gallery, a drawing room with painted windows of local historical figures, and a secret chamber in the Ivy Tower. Its octagonal conservatory was described as 'paved with Minton tiles, heated and ventilated in the best manner and filled with Exotic Plants'.

The sale of the property also included cellars, offices, estate cottages and private ways to the railway station and St John's Church. In spite of the estate agent's enthusiasm, ('the undulating formation of the Ground, and the old ruins and arches give a very picturesque effect') this was not enough for a would-be purchasers; the Castle did not reach its reserve price. Leach continued to live there, but he spent half the year in his villa on the Italian Riviera.

Although the Castle is a listed building, its interior has undergone various alterations over the years as new owners acquired the property. Sir Charles Rich bought the place in 1888 and spent a lot of money on a new billiard room; he also replaced the small Norman windows with large Tudor-style ones. In 1918 the property was bought by Ernest C Reed. More recently it was run as a Bed and Breakfast place and is now converted into flats.

POWERFUL POSITIONS - CASTLE AND CANAL

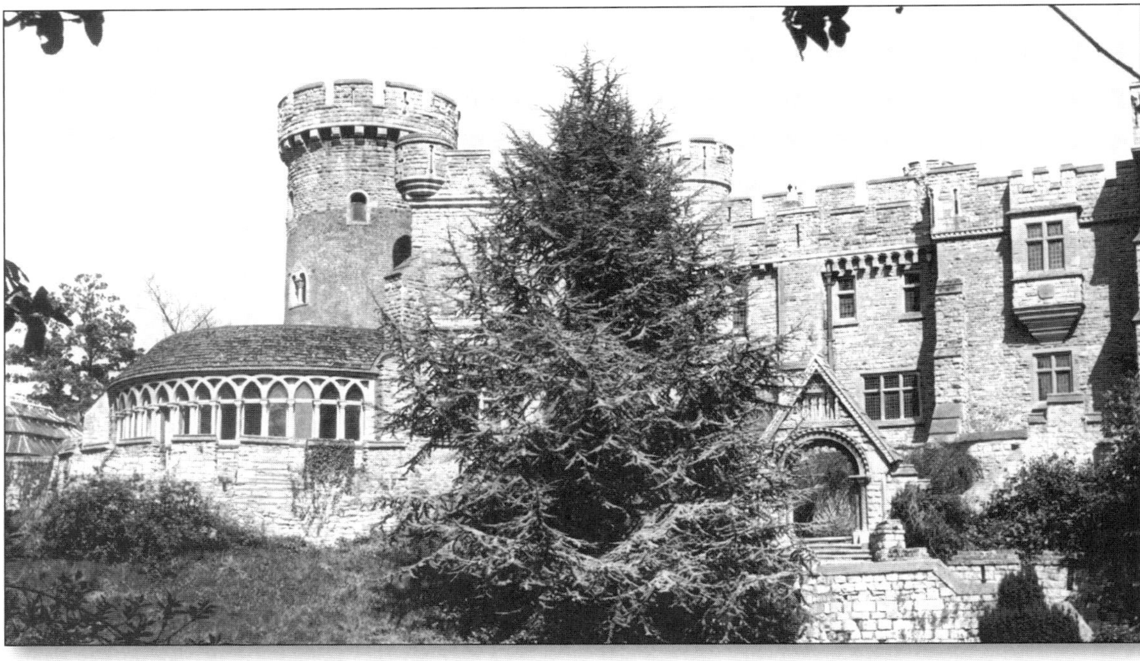

THE CASTLE c1955 D28047

This is a view from the south-east, and shows the Ladies' Gate on the right and the bowed fernery on the left. The brickwork of the original windmill can be seen on the Round Tower. To the far left we can just see the orangery. In the second view we are looking at the same façade as above, but from another angle; we can see details of the walls and windows.

THE CASTLE c1955 D28057

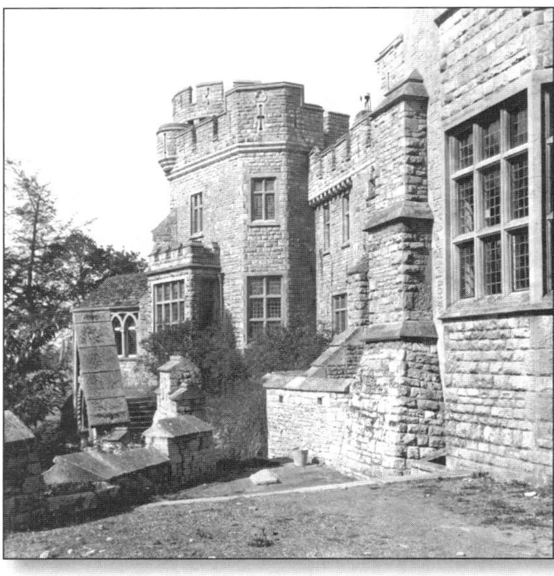

THE CASTLE TERRACE 1898 42310

It is fun to imagine who might have been sitting on the terrace on those rustic iron garden chairs before the Frith photographer arrived.

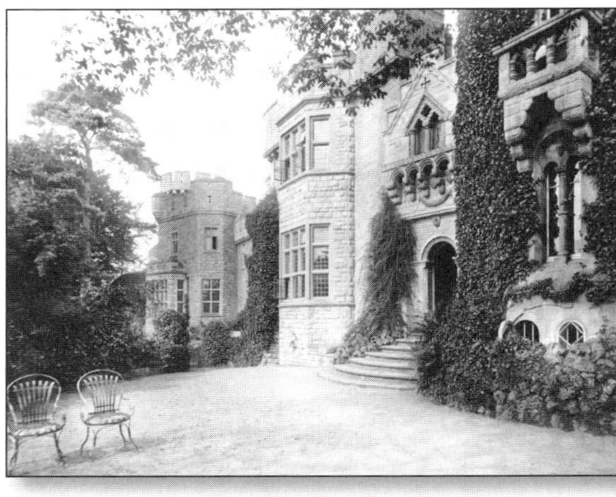

POWERFUL POSITIONS - CASTLE AND CANAL

Just as the Castle was once central to the town and its early status, so too was the canal. It was once a symbol of progress, as well as serving as a vital means of communication. For nearly half a century before the arrival of the railway, it provided the means for transporting heavy goods, vital for the economic growth of the town. When the railway line was completed, the canal was bought in 1852 by the company that eventually became the Great Western Railway.

Unfortunately, as its fortunes declined, so too did the canal's maintenance, and it was allowed to silt up. As road traffic increased, so the use of the canal decreased. The canal deteriorated so much that it was in danger of being closed altogether. Fortunately, locals cared sufficiently about its welfare to form the Kennet & Avon Canal Trust which petitioned parliament in 1956 against closure. It was a tremendous undertaking to restore the canal and its infrastructure. After many years of discussion, fund raising and cutting through red tape, work slowly progressed in different stages over the next twenty years.

In August 1990, the Queen re-opened the 87 miles of restored Kennet and Avon Canal, the second longest canal in the United Kingdom. This was a dream come true — now it was possible to travel from the River Thames at Reading to the River Avon at Bath in one continuous waterway. A huge crowd gathered at the top of the Caen Hill flight of locks to see Her Majesty board a boat and make a short journey to the next lock, which she named 'Queen Elizabeth II Lock'.

Whilst the restoration work had made the canal navigable, there were severe water storage problems, and structural problems still existed. The Caen Hill locks can now remain open to boats every day thanks to the £1 million new backpumping scheme to recycle water at the locks, completed in 1996, thus enabling 300,000 gallons of water to be lifted every hour to a height of 235 feet. The Kennet and Avon Canal Partnership recieved £25 million, one of the largest Heritage Lottery grants ever awarded, for their £29 million five-year plan of restoration work which was completed in 2003. HRH Prince Charles visited in May 2003 to celebrate this achievement.

The Kennet and Avon was originally built as three individual navigations. The Kennet Navigation opened in 1723, allowing boats to travel from Reading to Newbury. The River Avon was made navigable between Bath and Bristol in 1727. The 57-mile section which connected the two was completed in 1810. John Rennie, the Scottish-born engineer, designed and built it, including the construction of 29 locks in a space of just over two miles; these coped with the 237ft rise from the Avon valley to bring the canal to the town of Devizes. The total cost was just under £1million, which included the purchase of the Kennet Navigation and the obtaining of a controlling interest in the Avon Navigation.

The name 'Caen' is possibly a variation of 'cane'; the Rowde area was well known for its marshland and reed beds. Basket making was also a local industry. A 1721 map of the area shows a small section marked 'Cane Hill Acre'. When the canal was built, there were problems with the soft soil and sub-soil and withies, or bundles of willow, were used to line the canal bed.

For many locals, the canal was the life-blood of the town, both for commercial and social reasons. Some incidents reported in contemporary documents reflect this, usually when something illegal or tragic occurred. In his diary for 1807, George Sloper, the baker, wrote: 'July 10 — A boy — Smith — drowned in the new Cannall (near the bridge leading to New Park)'. Some of the reports of cases before the Devizes Divisional Sessions show punishments which seem very severe by today's standards: '1827 March 20 — Isaac Long of Devizes for an offence against Bye laws of the Canal Coy viz: unloading Coals over the 29th lock of the Canal. Fined £5, but failing to pay was committed for the House of Correction for 1 month'. Also, 'June 19 — John and William Pearce of Rowde for fishing in the Kennett & Avon Canal on June 4th. Convicted each in 40/-; on proof that they have no goods to distrain on, committed each for one calendar month'.

Today the Kennet & Avon Canal Trust can rightly be proud of the restoration work and the pleasure the canal and its environs give to people. Visitors can walk and cycle the tow paths easily, and travel by water with safety. There are regular trips from the Wharf, where the Trust museum and shop are housed. Anglers also know that they can fish legally in certain parts, and are not in danger of being sent to the House of Correction if they are found fishing in the pounds!

County Map

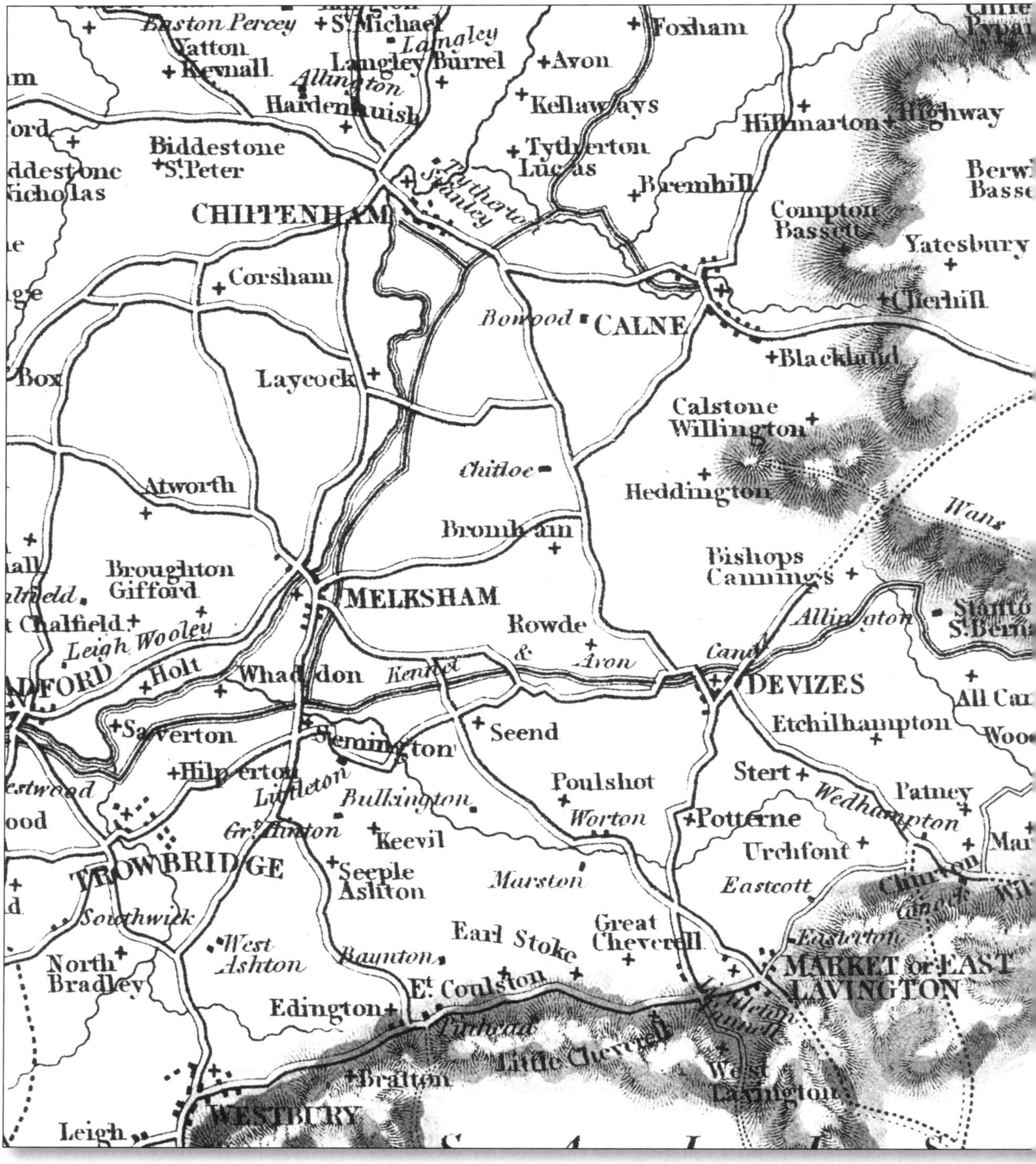

Easton Percey
St. Michael
Langley
Yatton
Kevnall
Langley Burrel
Allington
Avon
Foxham
Hardenhuish
Kellaways
Hillmarton
Highway
Biddestone
St. Peter
Tytherton
Lucas
Bremhill
CHIPPENHAM
Compton
Bassett
Yatesbury
Corsham
Cherhill
Bowood
CALNE
Blackland
Laycock
Calstone
Willington
Chitloe
Heddington
Atworth
Bromham
Broughton
Gifford
Bishops
Cannings
MELKSHAM
Rowde
Leigh Wooley
Holt
Whaddon
Kennet
&
Avon
DEVIZES
Etchilhampton
Seend
Semington
Poulshot
Stert
Patney
Littleton
Bulkington
Worton
Potterne
Keevil
Urchfont
TROWBRIDGE
Seeple
Ashton
Marston
Eastcott
Southwick
West
Ashton
Earl Stoke
Great
Cheverell
North
Bradley
Baynton
MARKET or EAST
LAVINGTON
Edington
Et. Coulston
Tinhead
Little Cheverell
Bratton
West
Lavington
WESTBURY
Leigh

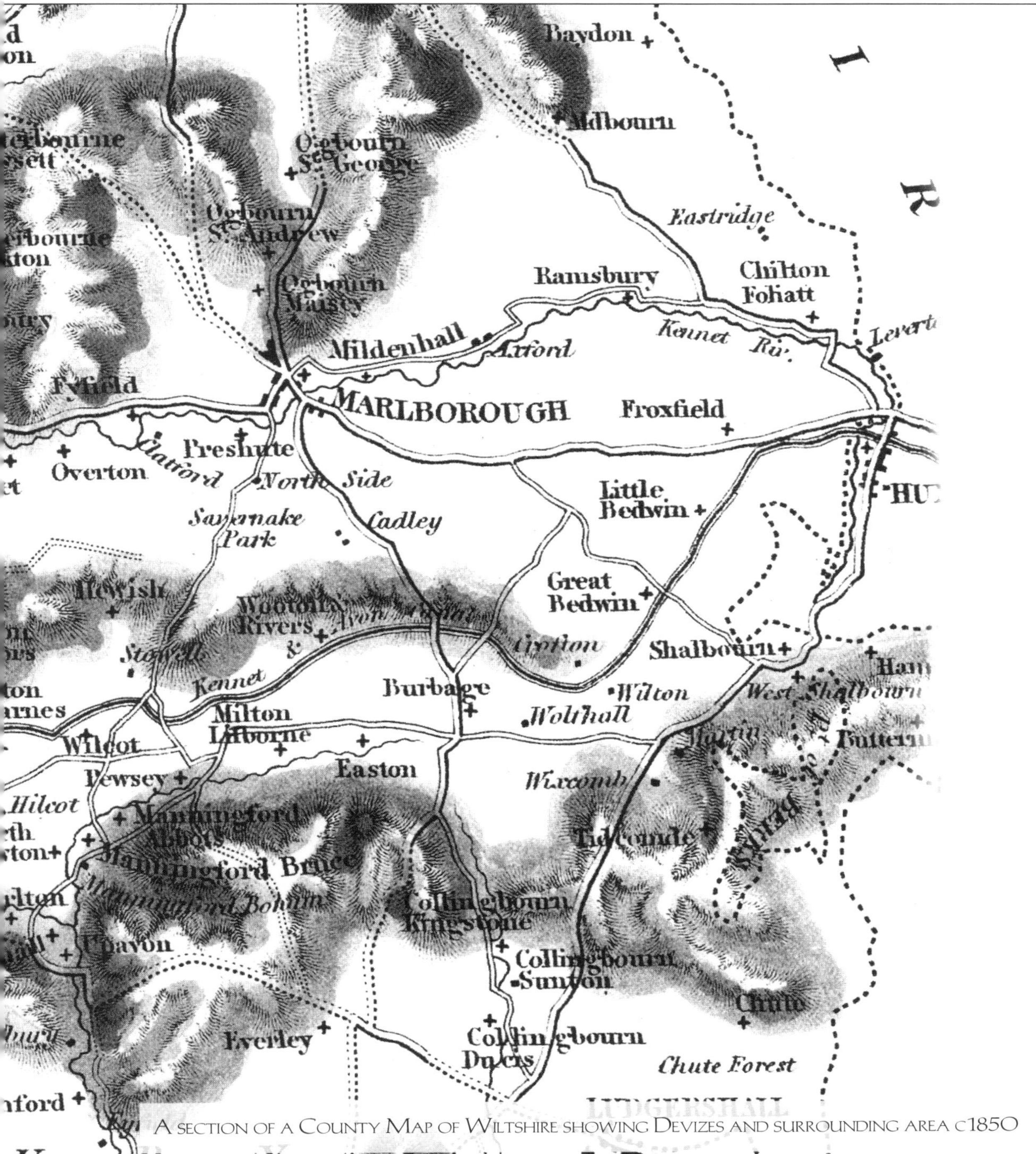

A SECTION OF A COUNTY MAP OF WILTSHIRE SHOWING DEVIZES AND SURROUNDING AREA C1850

POWERFUL POSITIONS - CASTLE AND CANAL

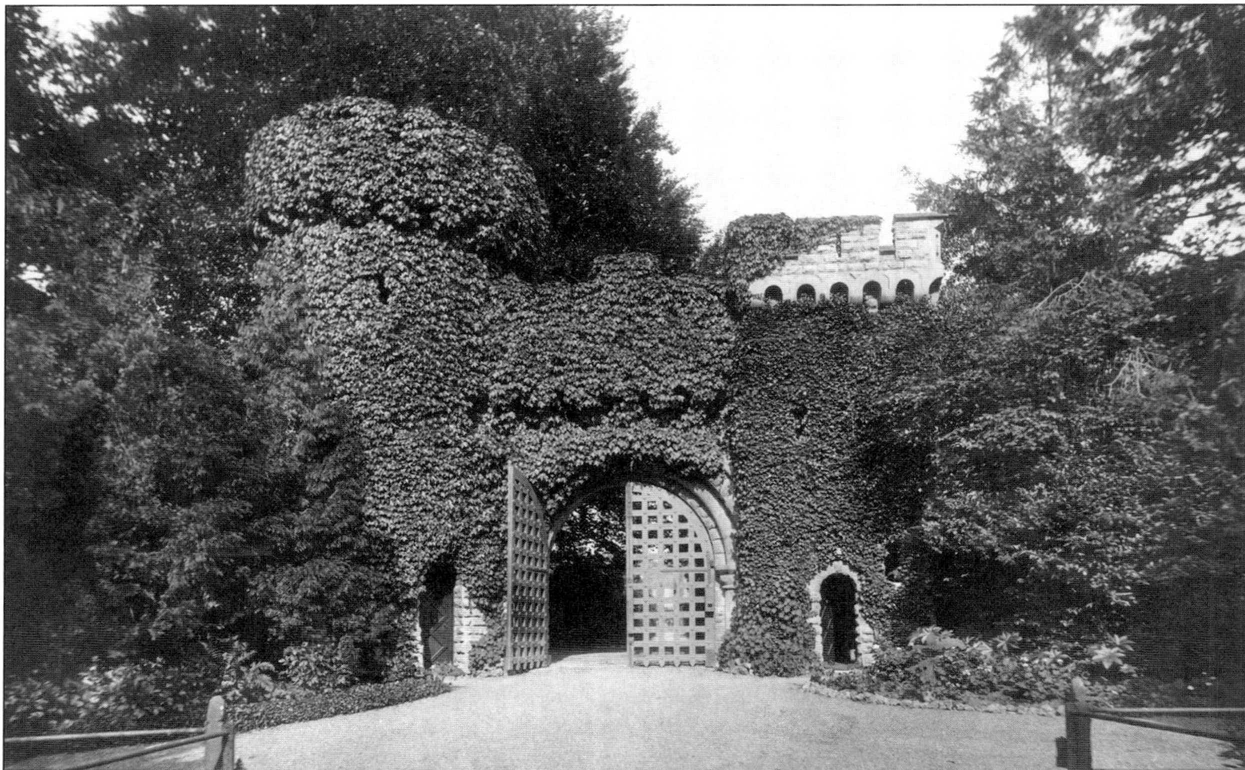

Above: Devizes, The Castle Gatehouse 1898 42307

Ivy and creeper cover the attractive features of what is known as the Town Gate or Castle Lodge. It is described in the Department of the Environment List of Special Architectural or Historic Interest: 'Large round tower and lower square tower flanking gateway with machicolated crenellated parapets. The double grid pattern timber gates are set in large Norman archway, flanked by heavy shafts with cushion capitals'. What has changed today is the addition of a bungalow built into the body of the square tower.

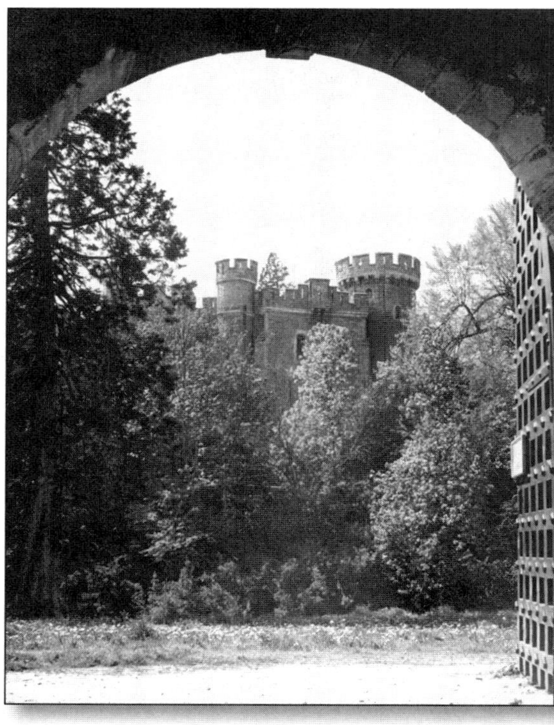

The Castle c1955 D28046

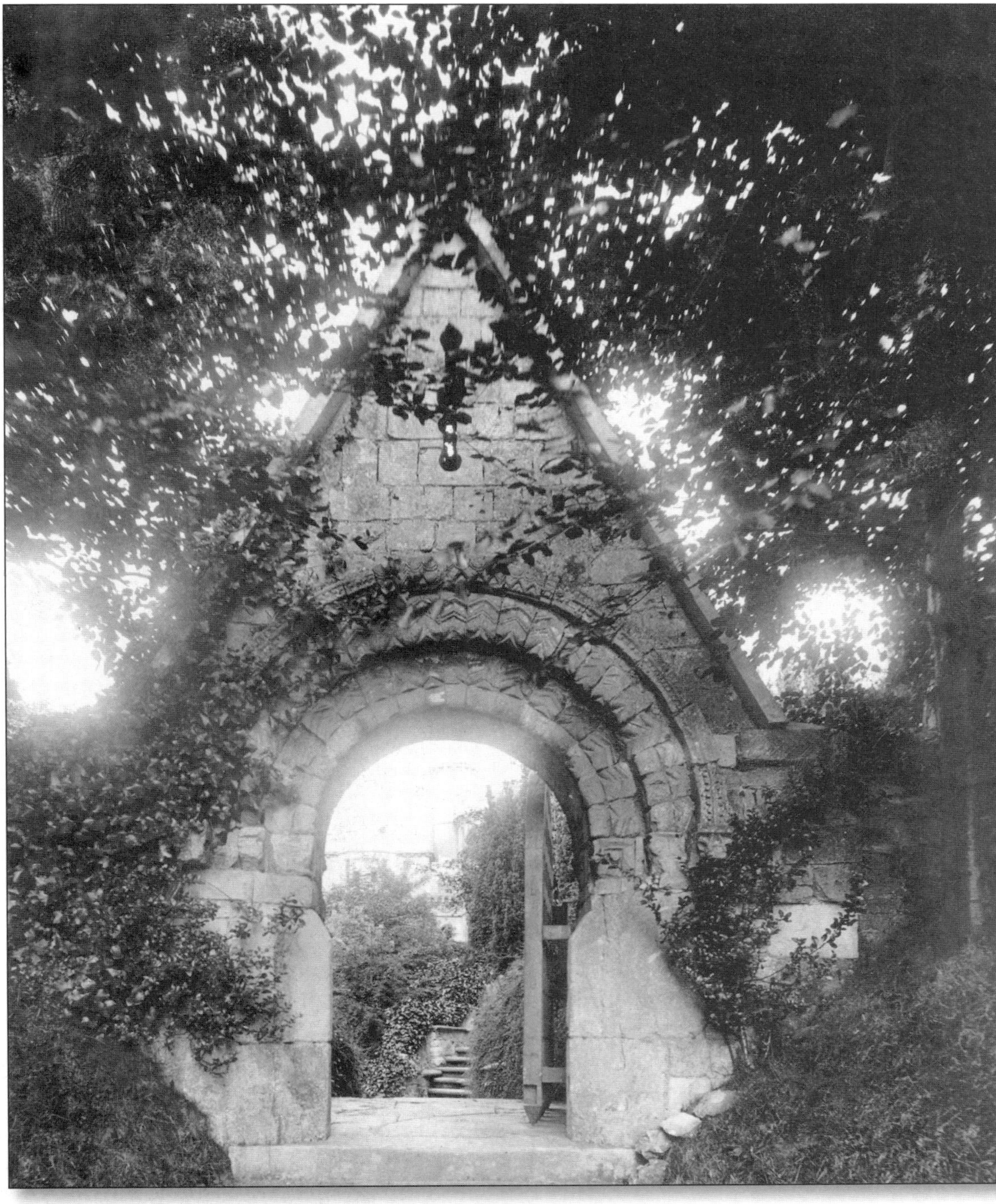

THE CASTLE, BISHOP'S GATE 1898 42311

This is also known as St John's Gate and is thought to incorporate a stone arch taken from the Norman church of St John. Notice the zigzag stone work on the arch which is typical of that period.

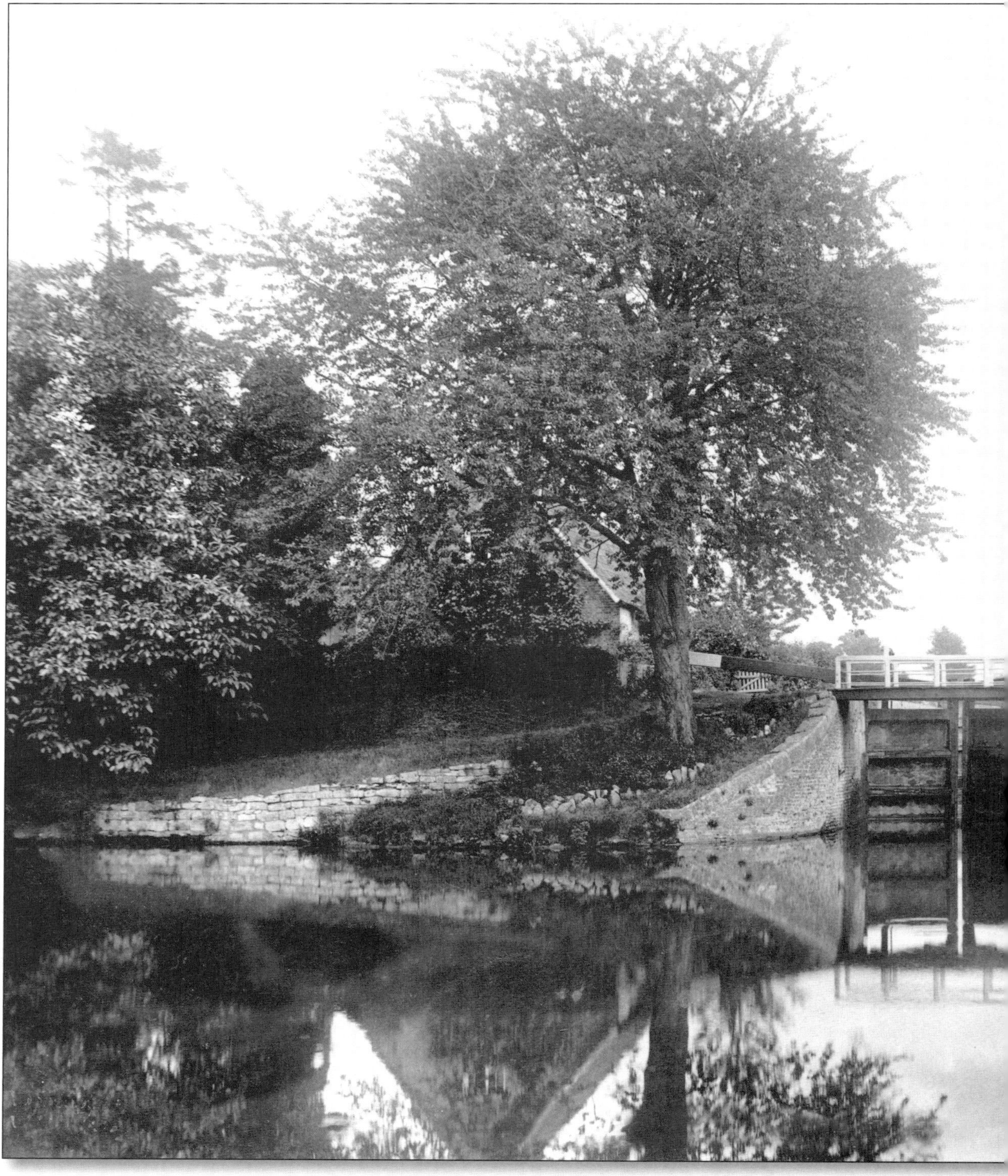

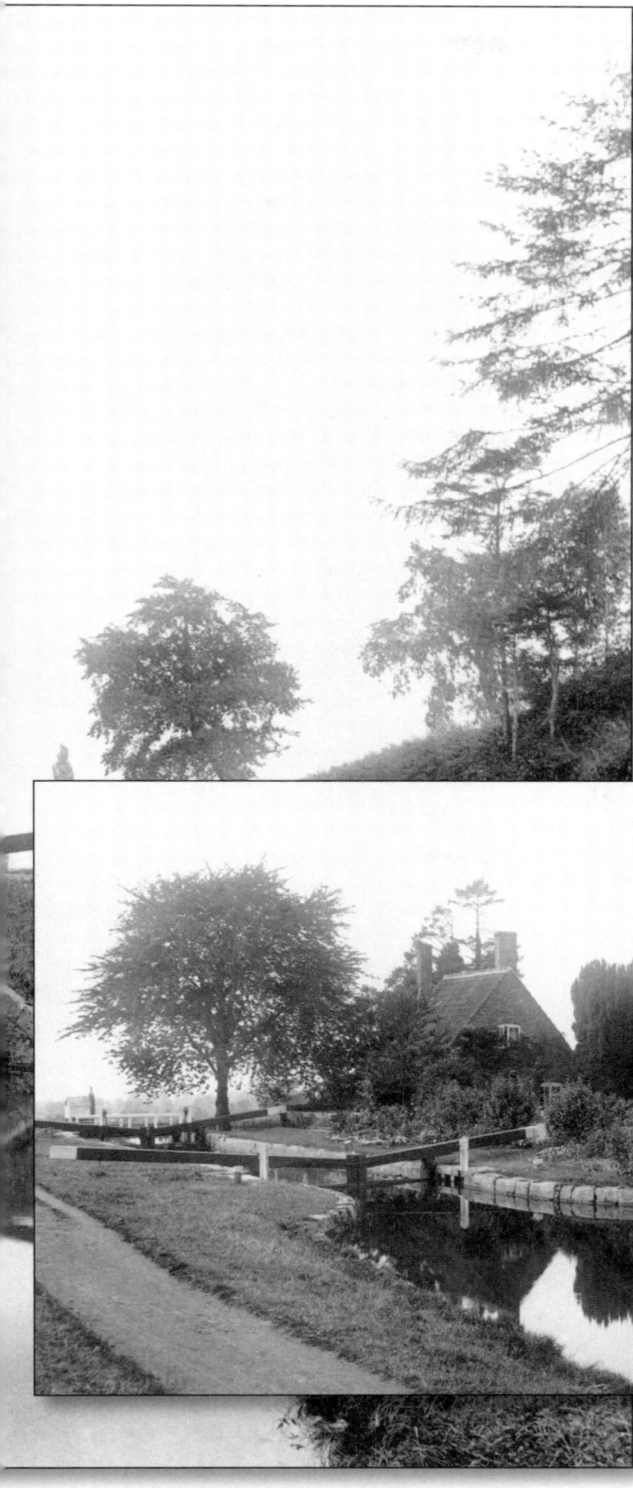

Left: THE CANAL AND THE LOCK 1898 42319

Taken from Lock 43 looking towards Devizes, this photograph shows Lock 44 and a cottage, and also one of the pounds — a pound is an area for the storage of water.

Below: ON THE CANAL 1898 42318

This shows the lock-keeper's cottage at Lock 44. Behind it can be seen the roof of the Canal Company's workshop, now occupied by British Waterways, who maintain the canal today. The cottage now houses a tea room.

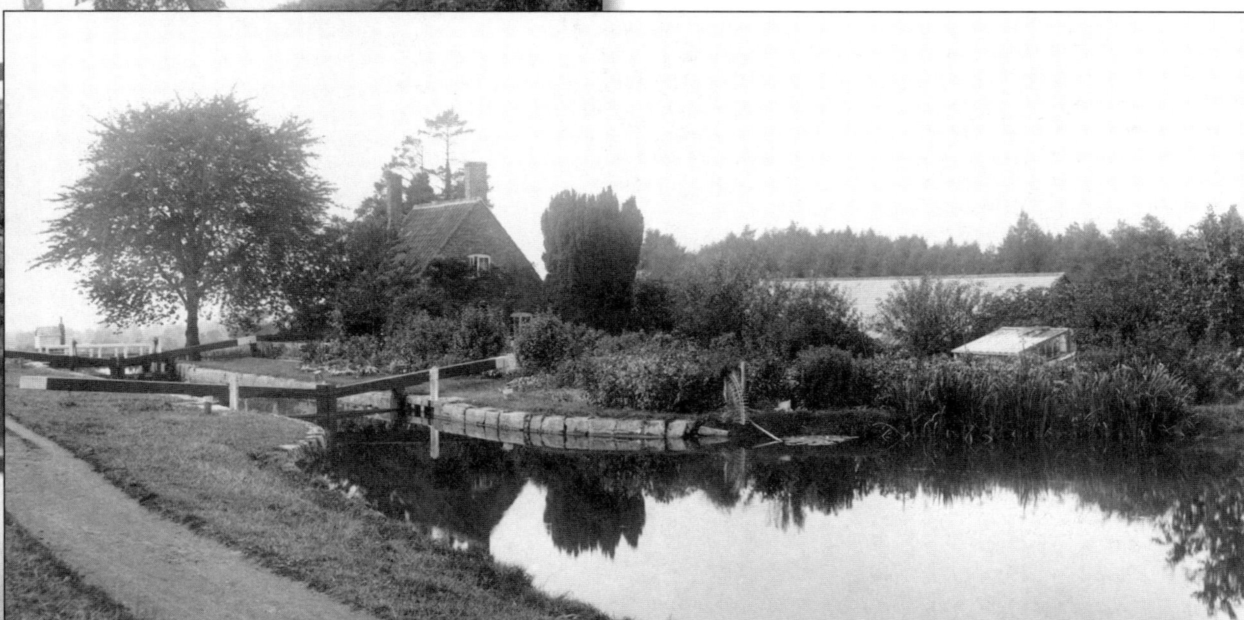

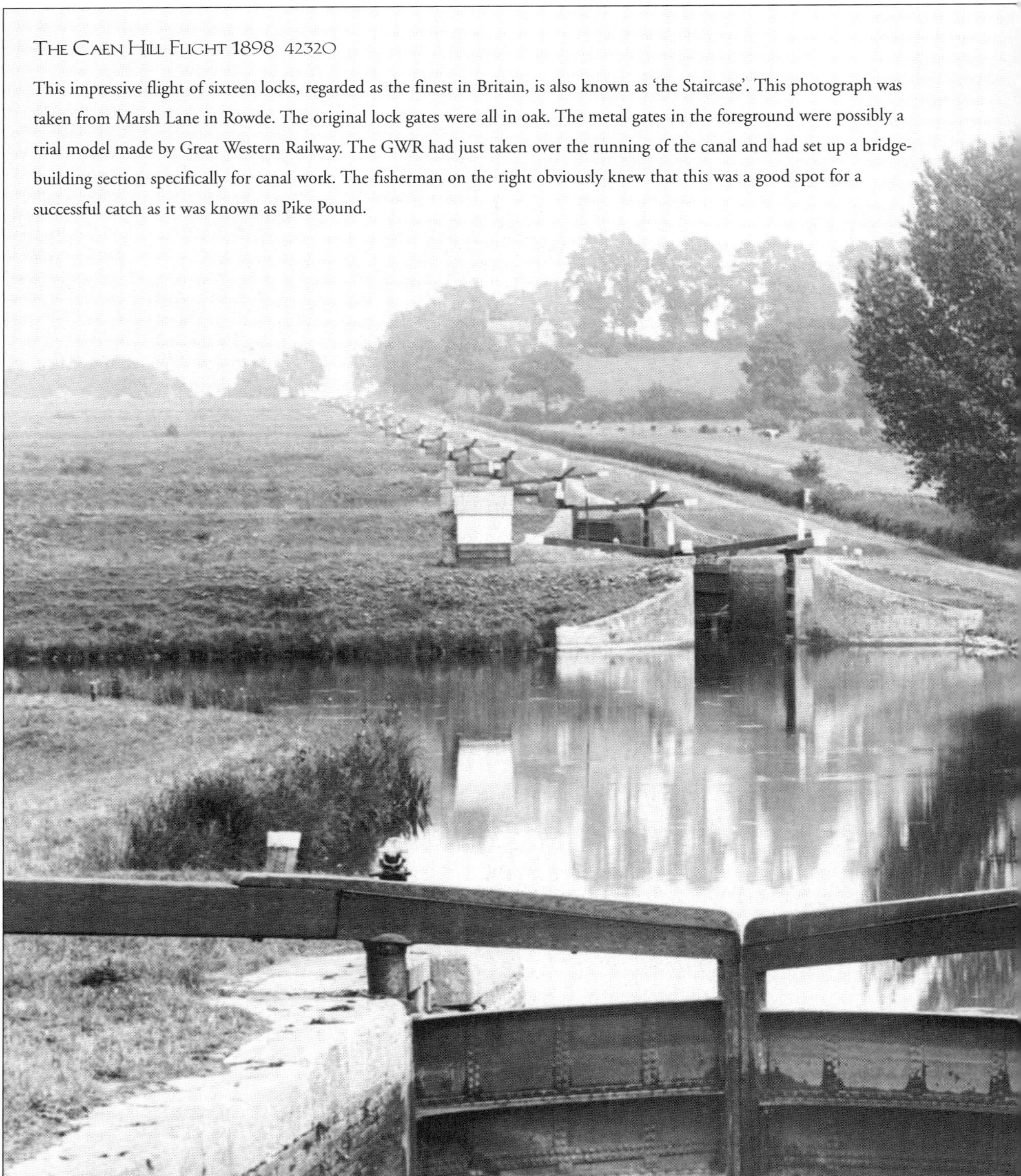

THE CAEN HILL FLIGHT 1898 42320

This impressive flight of sixteen locks, regarded as the finest in Britain, is also known as 'the Staircase'. This photograph was taken from Marsh Lane in Rowde. The original lock gates were all in oak. The metal gates in the foreground were possibly a trial model made by Great Western Railway. The GWR had just taken over the running of the canal and had set up a bridge-building section specifically for canal work. The fisherman on the right obviously knew that this was a good spot for a successful catch as it was known as Pike Pound.

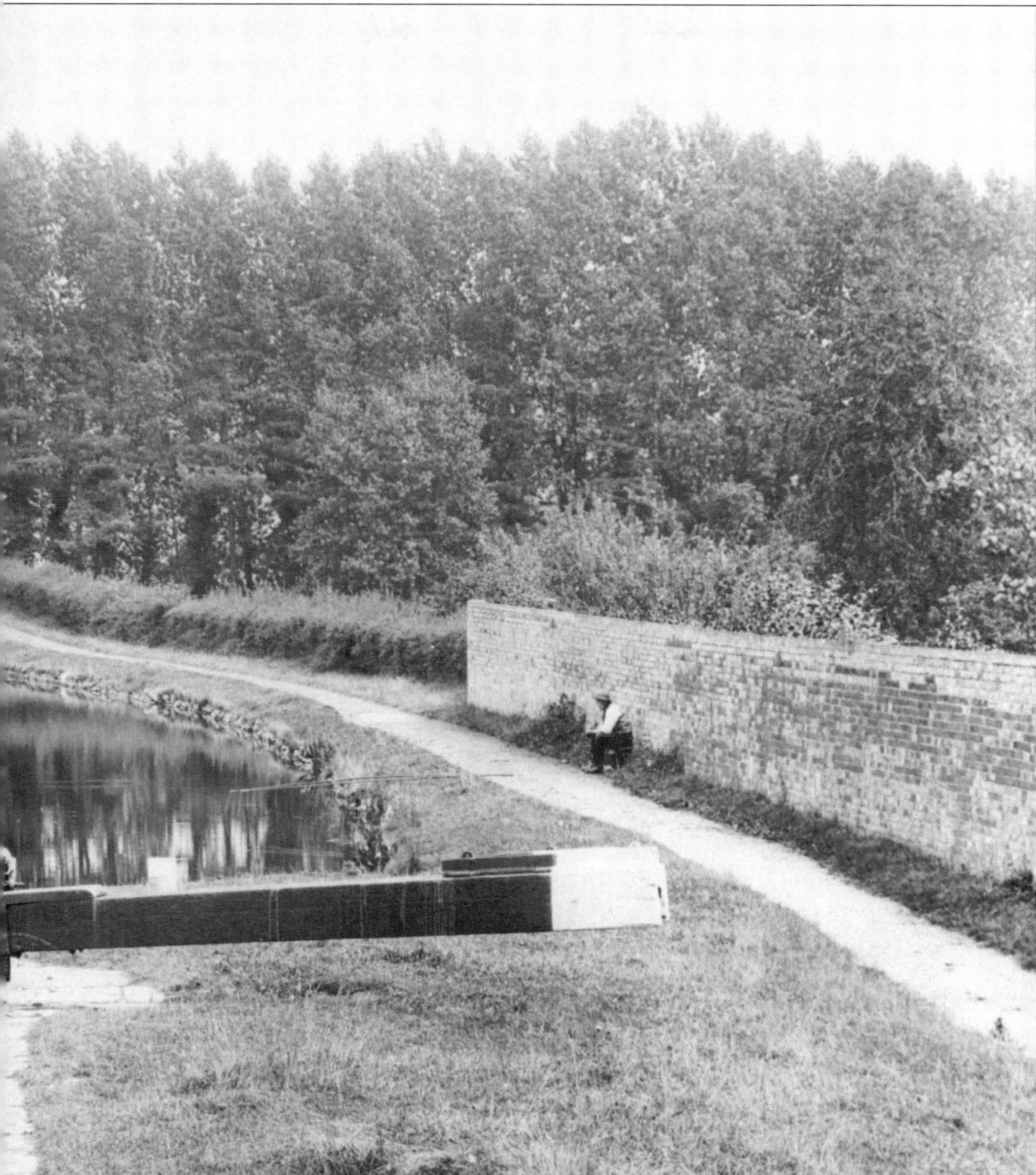

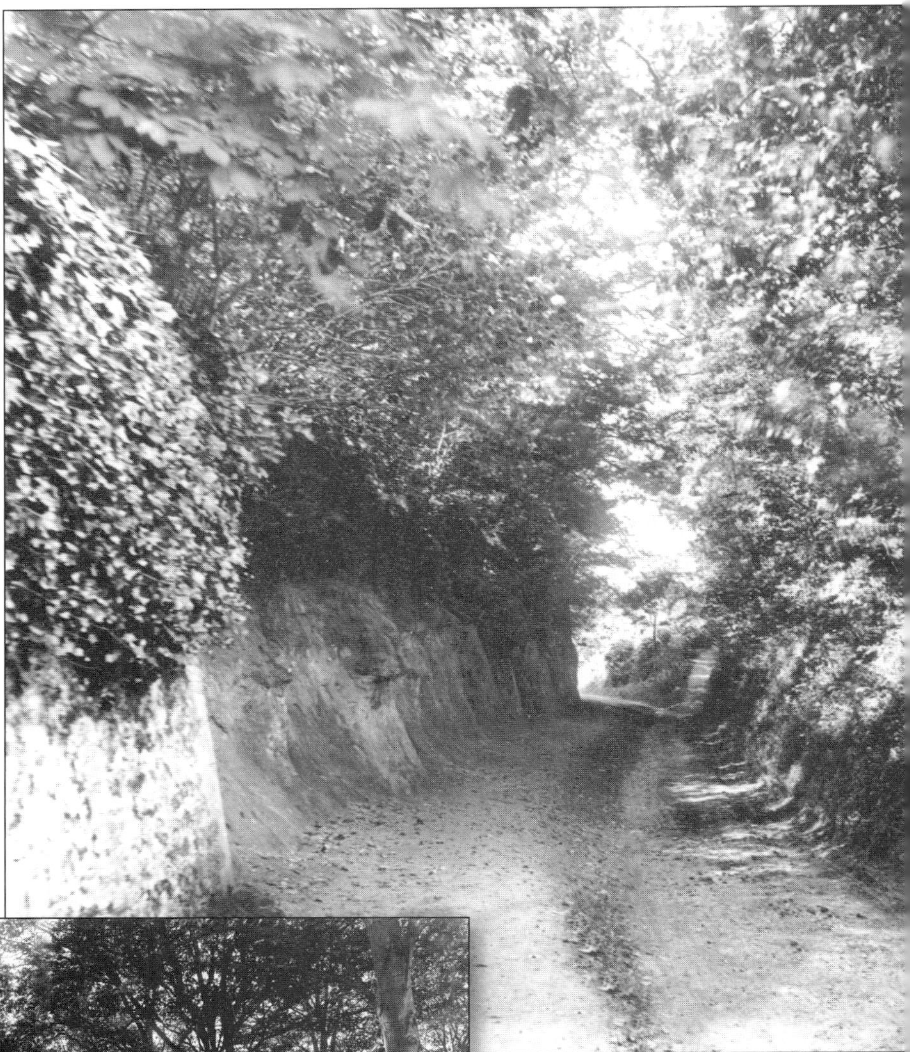

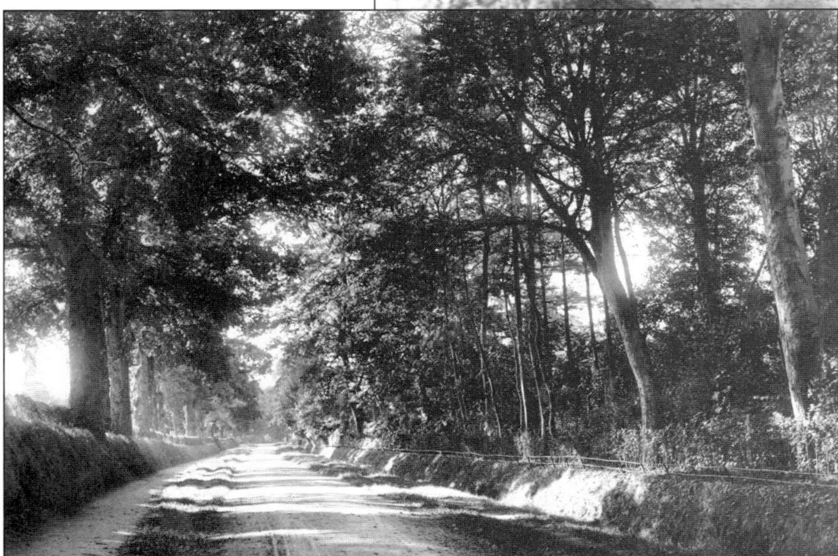

Above: HARTMOOR 1898 42326

In 'Mates Illustrated Guide' of 1906, the area is described as 'very steady and pretty with good views but muddy in damp weather'. The area still retains much of this rural charm with its canopy of trees and ancient hedgerows.

Left: HARTMOOR 1899 44847

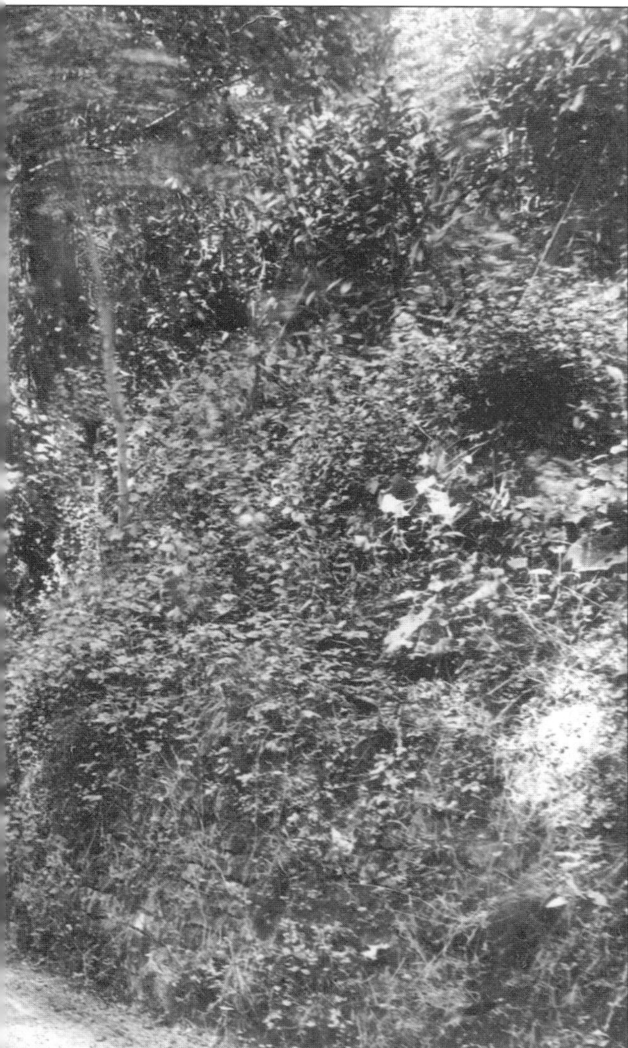

Hartmoor Road used to be the main route between the Castle and the Bishop of Salisbury's possessions at Potterne. It was known as the Devizes Sandway in the 17th century. Until the early 18th century it was the main thoroughfare to Potterne and the coach road to Five Lanes. In the 19th century it was also known as 'Prize Bandway', a play on the earlier name.

Hartmoor has long been a local beauty spot, and in spite of road surfacing and housing development along some parts, it remains much the same. The trees and hedges still grow luxuriantly. Tractors and Landrovers are a familiar sight on the road as they travel to and from the local farms.

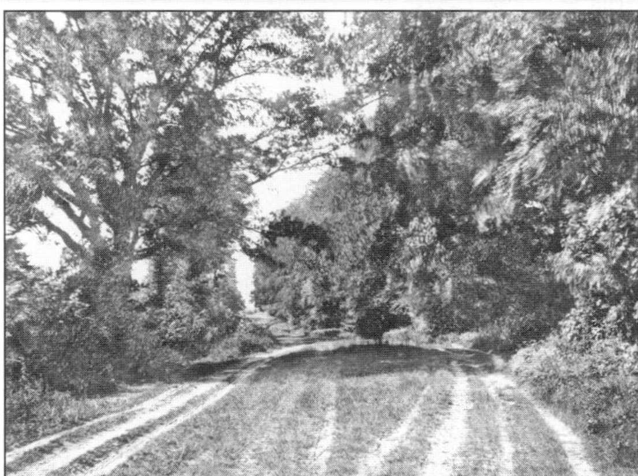

HARTMOOR 1898 42327

OUT AND ABOUT - AROUND DEVIZES

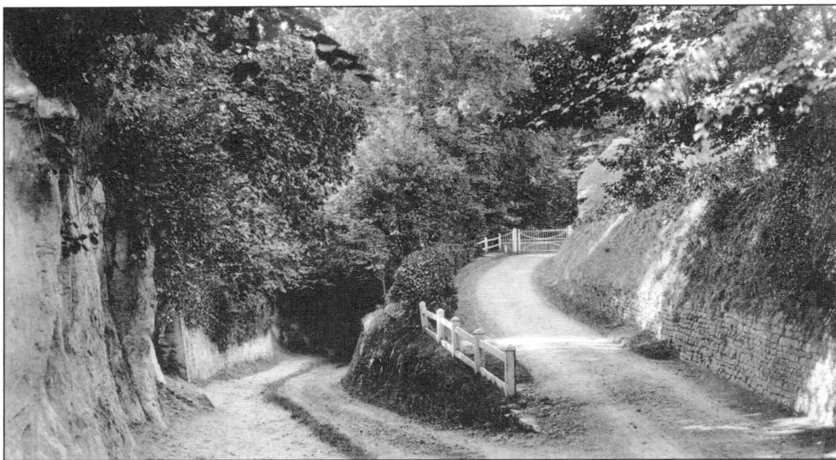

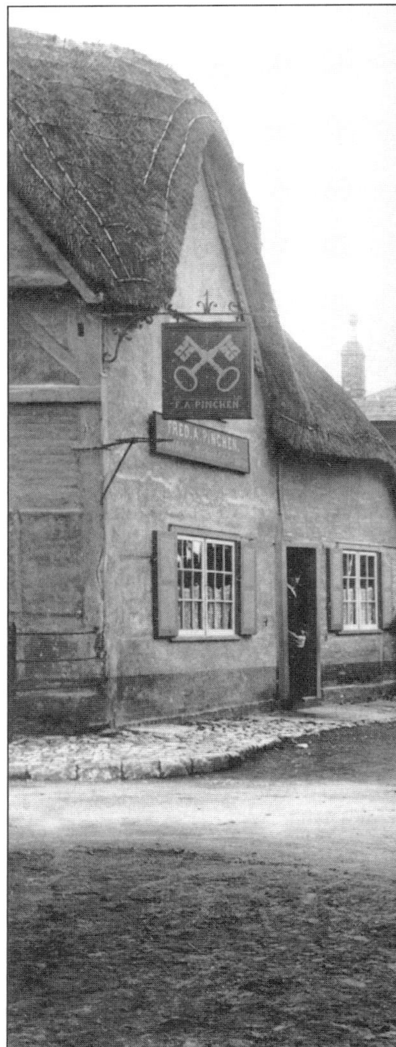

Above: HARTMOOR 1899 44846

East Lodge can just be glimpsed at the entrance to the drive from Hartmoor Road which leads to Old Park House. It is a listed building and is described as '2 storeys, rough cast on brick with thatch roof, the eaves swept down on west side to form veranda with flint and rubble columns'.

Below Left: DREW'S POND 1899 44848

This idyllic scene could be taken straight out of a Hardy novel. Unfortunately, the cottage was demolished in 1960. The pond is on the right, hidden by the trees.

Below Right: DUNKIRK HILL 1903 49899

This shows a very deserted unmade road leading into town, more familiar to motorists today, who have to slow down at the top in order to join the Bath Road into Devizes. Over the years the foliage and the soil on both sides has been cut back to keep the problem of earth slippage under control.

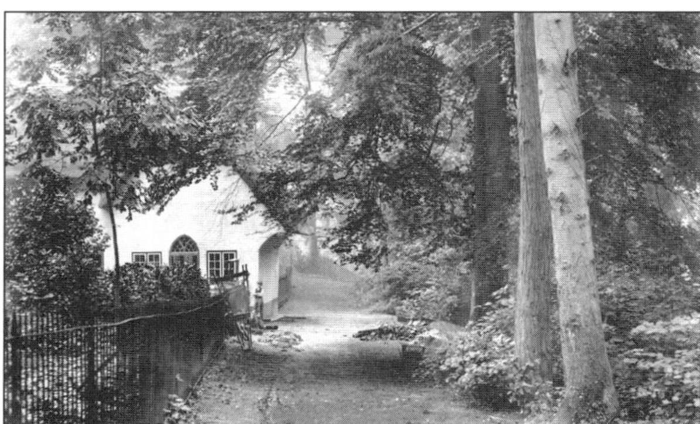

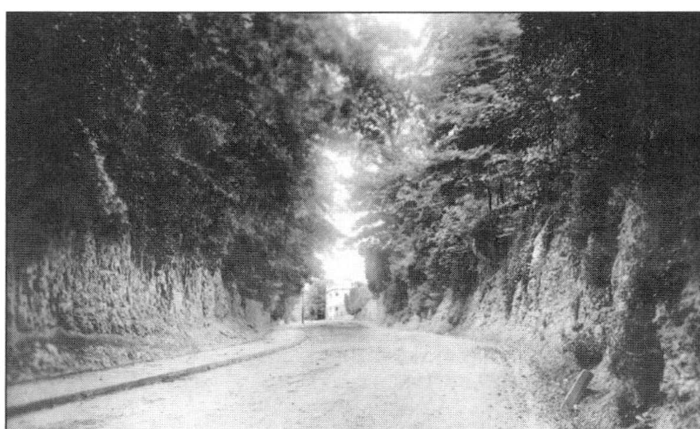

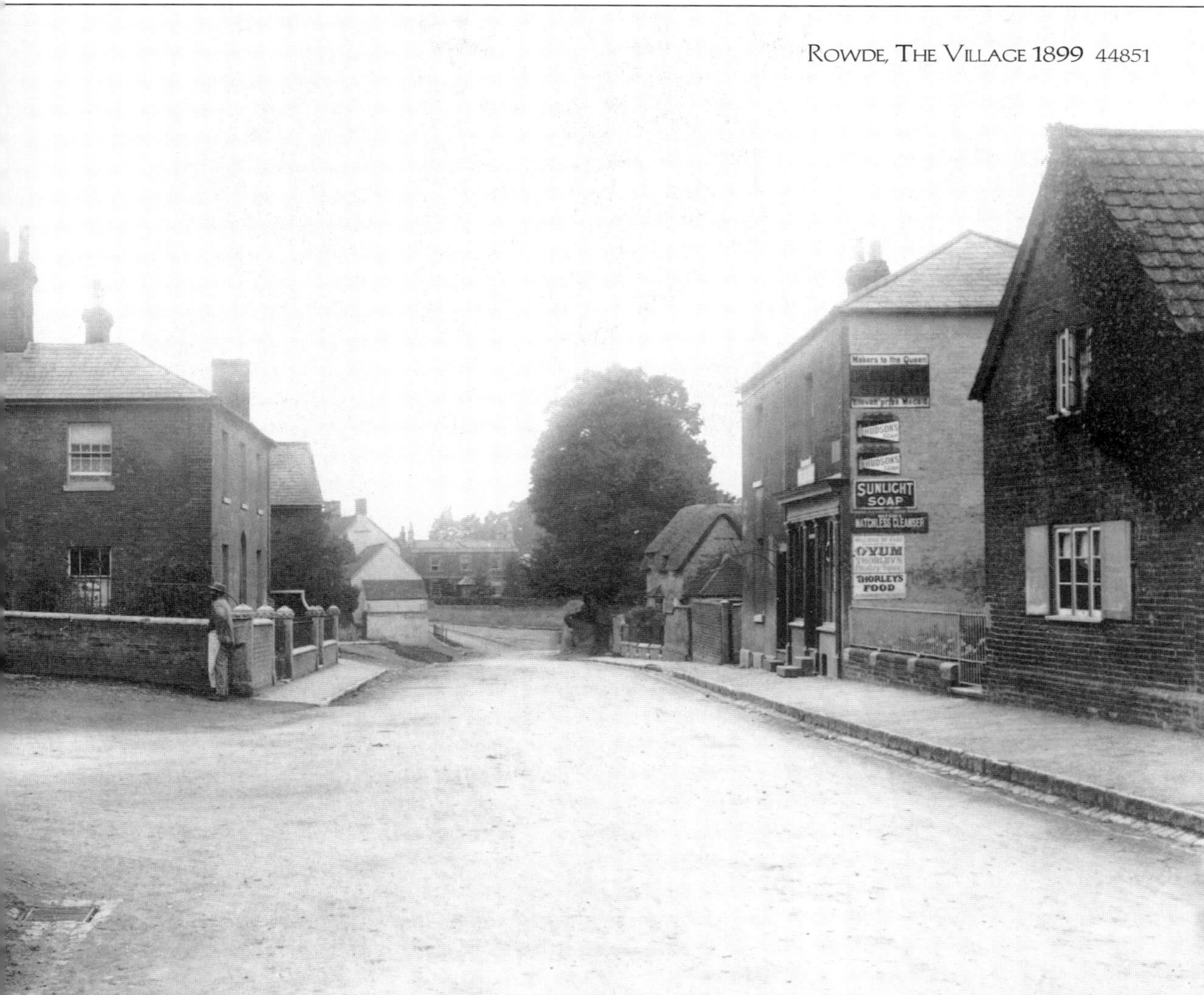

ROWDE, THE VILLAGE 1899 44851

Drew's Pond (44848) and the surrounding area have always been popular with locals. Unfortunately, it was the scene of a tragedy one Sunday in June in 1751 when five people, including a bride and groom, were drowned while boating. A 15ft-high obelisk in St John's churchyard commemorates the deaths. The admonitory words 'Remember the Sabbath to keep it holy' and 'Remember thy Creator in the days of thy youth' were thought suitable for the inscription. In spite of the many changes to the area, including housing developments, there is a beautiful woodland trail here, which is popular with walkers.

The Bath Road out of Devizes branches off to Chippenham at Shane's Castle, an old toll house (49899, centre). Pevsner describes it as 'small and generously castellated'. Dunkirk Hill was formerly known as Rowde Hill. Road improvements in the 18th century were paid for from tolls collected at various entrances to the town.

Rowde is about a mile and a half from Devizes and six miles from Calne. It is an attractive little village, and used to be on the main coach route to Salisbury. It was a popular stopping-off place for travellers, and the three local inns did good business. The Cross Keys and the George and Dragon still survive, but the Lamb Inn was demolished.

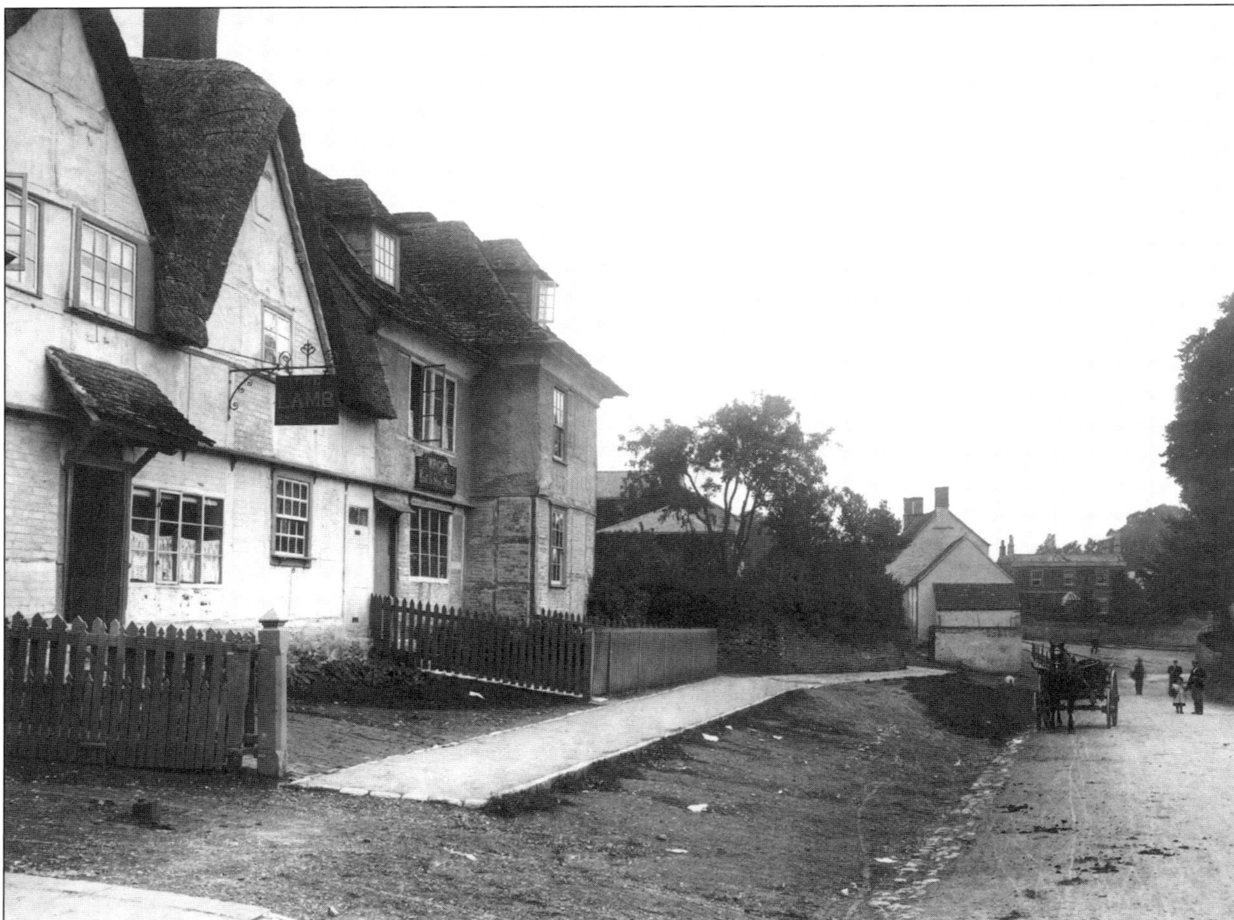

ROWDE, THE VILLAGE 1899 44850

The thatched building on the left is early 17th-century wattle and daub with some brick infill, and was an alehouse called the Lamb. Adjoining it was a boot maker, and the projecting part was a separate residence.

The Cross Keys on the left (in 44851, page 85) was destroyed by fire in 1937 and rebuilt in its present form, unthatched. The large house next to it was variously a private residence, a working men's club and also the Post Office before it moved opposite. It is now part of the Cross Keys car park. The Post Office and general stores on the right also had a bakery at the back, and still has today. At the time of this picture, there were about six bakeries in a village with a population of 878. The owners made full use of the side of the building to advertise some of their lines.

The Lamb was demolished in the 1960s to make way for Maundrell Close, a small development of houses built where former weavers' cottages once stood. The remainder of the house is now a listed building. The George and Dragon can be seen on the bend of the road to the left of the horse and cart in 44850.

Cars still travel this road, just as the old coaches did. People still visit the public houses for refreshment much as the weary and dusty travellers did a hundred years ago. This village and the area surrounding Devizes is fortunate in having preserved much of its past in its buildings, roads and waterways. The photographs and postcards in private and public collections also help to remind us of our heritage and to keep alive memories of a past age.

INDEX

Names of Pre-Publication Buyers

The following people have kindly supported this book by purchasing limited edition copies prior to publication.

Tom and Amanda, 13th August 2005

Beryl Arnold

Canon and Mrs John Ayers

David Billett

In memory of Phyllis Blackmore of Rowde

To my son Paul Blake, love Mum

Peter Bowerbank

To our Granddaughter Caitlin, with love

Carol Keeler

John and Jennifer Chowney, Devizes

Gillian and Alan Coggins

Patricia Coldrick 11-10-05

Mr B P A and Mrs K R Daines

The Davey Family, Devizes

Lynn and David, Rowde, Devizes

S D and the late K G Diskett, Devizes

A E Duffall, J A Dufall, Devizes

The Edwards Family, Urchfont

The Eva Family, Devizes

In memory of the Rowels and Ferris Families, Devizes

Ronald and Joyce Ferris, Manor Farm, Rowde

The Field Family

Isobel and Bruce Fishlock of Devizes

The Ford Family

The Giddings Family, Devizes and Urchfont

In loving memory of Fredric H G Goddard

Mr William Goddard

Joanna Gorsuch

Peter J Gough, Devizes

The Green Family

Mr E Grist, Mrs M Grist, Devizes

Steven and June Harris, Easterton

Richard Harris, Happy Birthday 9/9/05

James Henderson

T J W Henly, Devizes

Peter James Hibberd

Dave and Dawn Holland's 1st Anniversary

The Holmes Family, Devizes

Marion Humphries, Born Devizes 1939

Mr J G and Mrs A G Hurst, Devizes

Sheila Hurst

In memory of Gordon A Jackson, Devizes

The Jackson Family from Rowde, now all over UK

To Mum and Dad, hope you enjoy this, lots of love, Jo

D P Johnson

Mrs Jacqueline Eileen Jones

Barry Anthony King

Remembered, Fred Kirby, Mayor and Freeman

Mr Mervyn Charles Knight

Mr and Mrs Don Macmillan, Etchilhampton

To my dear wife, Margaret, from John, 2005

Charles Masey

Mr Jeffery Matthews and Family, Devizes

The Matthews Family, Rowde

The McCann Family, Devizes

Nanette McCaughey, formerly of Devizes

A F and L Mills, Devizes

Mrs J Moore, née Bartlett, In memory of Mum and Dad

Peter and Ann Morris, Newcomers to Devizes

Jan and Rich Oakman

The Parkins Family, Devizes

To Dad John Pearce on his Birthday, from Mary

In memory of Allan James Penfold, Worton, Devizes

For Mum and Dad from M G and J E Pitcher

Colin D Ramsay, Devizes

Paul Reardon, Shirley Reardon, Devizes

To May Redding, love from Jayne

Mr and Mrs G J Reeves

John and Olivia Roberts, W.A.

The Rossiter Family

Mr A J and Mrs P R S Sampson

Natalie J Samways, Devizes

Mr and Mrs C Sault

In memory of Lauraine Scammell, Poulshot

Donald J Sherrard, Manton and West Lavington

To Helen Janice Shirley, on her birthday

Joe Slattery, Devizes

Michael J Stretton, Potterne

Mrs Margaret and Mr Ray Taylor, Devizes

Sue and Maurice Taylor, in their Ruby Wedding year

Laura and James Thomas, from GM and GD

To Grandma June, from James and Thomas

Jill Vaughan, BSC, MSC of Devizes

Philip and Vera Wadman

Mr J P Walter, Potterne, Devizes

Ady and Chele on our Wedding Day

Phil and Karen West, Devizes 2004

To Barbara Wilton on your birthday,
from Roger and Anne

Mr and Mrs Wray, Potterne, Wiltshire

Clive Humphries and Debbie Wright

Frith Products & Services

Francis Frith would doubtless be pleased to know that the pioneering publishing venture he started in 1860 still continues today. Over a hundred and forty years later, The Francis Frith Collection continues in the same innovative tradition and is now one of the foremost publishers of vintage photographs in the world. Some of the current activities include:

Interior Decoration

Today Frith's photographs can be seen framed and as giant wall murals in thousands of pubs, restaurants, hotels, banks, retail stores and other public buildings throughout the country. In every case they enhance the unique local atmosphere of the places they depict and provide reminders of gentler days in an increasingly busy and frenetic world.

Product Promotions

Frith products are used by many major companies to promote the sales of their own products or to reinforce their own history and heritage. Frith promotions have been used by Hovis bread, Courage beers, Scots Porage Oats, Colman's mustard, Cadbury's foods, Mellow Birds coffee, Dunhill pipe tobacco, Guinness, and Bulmer's Cider.

Genealogy and Family History

As the interest in family history and roots grows world-wide, more and more people are turning to Frith's photographs of Great Britain for images of the towns, villages and streets where their ancestors lived; and, of course, photographs of the churches and chapels where their ancestors were christened, married and buried are an essential part of every genealogy tree and family album.

Frith Products

All Frith photographs are available Framed or just as Mounted Prints and Posters (size 23 x 16 inches). These may be ordered from the address below. From time to time other products - Address Books, Calendars, Table Mats, etc - are available.

The Internet

Already ninety thousand Frith photographs can be viewed and purchased on the internet through the Frith websites and a myriad of partner sites.

For more detailed information on Frith companies and products, look at these sites:

www.francisfrith.co.uk
www.francisfrith.com
(for North American visitors)

See the complete list of Frith Books at:

www.francisfrith.co.uk

This web site is regularly updated with the latest list of publications from The Francis Frith Collection. If you wish to buy books relating to another part of the country that your local bookshop does not stock, you may purchase on-line.

For further information, trade, or author enquiries please contact us at the address below:

The Francis Frith Collection, Frith's Barn, Teffont, Salisbury, Wiltshire, England SP3 5QP.
Tel: +44 (0)1722 716 376 Fax: +44 (0)1722 716 881 Email: sales@francisfrith.co.uk

See Frith books on the internet at www.francisfrith.co.uk